PEARSON

ALWAYS LEARNING

Fresh Voices:
Composition at Cal Poly

2012–2013
Volume VI

Editor
Brenda Helmbrecht, Director of Writing

Assistant Editors
Jon Bartel
Sadie Johann

Editors
Leticia Ericson
Rebekah Maples

Pearson Learning Solutions, 501 Boylston Street, Suite 900, Boston, MA 02116
A Pearson Education Company
www.pearsoned.com

Printed in the United States of America

1 2 3 4 5 6 7 8 9 10 V363 17 16 15 14 13 12

000200010271697996

BW

ISBN 10: 1-256-82762-2
ISBN 13: 978-1-256-82762-7

Contents

Appendices 107

Letter from the Director of Writing

Very few writers really know what they are doing until they've done it.

—*from Anne Lamott's* Bird by Bird

Dear Student:

Welcome to the sixth volume of *Fresh Voices*, a collection of writing that showcases the effort, commitment, and talent of last year's English 133 and 134 students.

The essays featured in the collection are typical of the intellectual engagement promoted in Cal Poly's first-year writing classes. We value the work of these writers because they took sophisticated approaches to the same assignments you are likely to meet in your composition course. They explored issues that mattered to them—and they used unique and interesting rhetorical strategies to engage their readers. These essays each have a distinct voice and style. Thus, we think these writers have something to teach you about writing at Cal Poly.

The selection committee and I did not select these essays because they earned "As" or because they are perfect (frankly, we don't know what grades these essays received—neither does your instructor). Moreover, our intention is not for you to imitate these essays. Instead, read the essays in this collection with an eye toward your own writing. Ask yourself, "What can I learn from these students' rhetorical choices?" The essays in this collection will offer you new ways to approach your writing, perhaps in terms of how to craft an introduction, how to integrate quotations, or even how to develop and support your essay's thesis. Most importantly, these essays can help you bring greater complexity and depth to your writing—two traits that are highly valued in our composition courses.

At the end of the collection, you will find important information about writing at Cal Poly. For instance, we have included information about campus resources that can provide additional support with your writing and research, including the University Writing and Rhetoric Center and Kennedy Library, as well as your instructor's office hours. I also encourage you to become familiar with the "Defining and Avoiding Plagiarism" section. And finally, at the end of collection, you will find information for submitting your work to next year's *Fresh Voices*.

As the Director of Writing at Cal Poly, my job is to ensure that you receive progressive and innovative approaches to writing instruction. Indeed, one of Cal Poly's stated University Learning Objectives (ULO) is "effective communication," which means that you will be developing your writing skills throughout your Cal Poly career. You will soon find that writing at the college level requires you to not only demonstrate mastery of the skills you developed in high school, but also to develop new approaches to writing that you may not have tried before.

In my experience directing the writing program and teaching composition at Cal Poly, I have noted that students who stick with their "old" methods of writing—despite what they are learning in their college classes—tend to struggle the most in ENGL 133 and 134. For instance, you will be asked to write essays that move beyond the five-paragraph structure—or other formulaic approaches to writing—you may have encountered in high school. You will be expected to select an organizational strategy that suits your topic, to use language and punctuation that most effectively conveys your meaning, to address your audience appropriately, and to select essay topics you care about.

Therefore, I encourage you to:

- take advantage of the opportunity to revise.
- spend time with your instructor's carefully considered feedback.
- dismiss the notion that you "write" best under the pressure of time constraints.
- be prepared to receive assessments of your writing that are different in tone and purpose than the feedback you received in high school.
- keep an open mind.

In short, you will be held accountable for the choices you make as a writer.

Perhaps you have been waiting to exercise some creative control over your own writing. If you commit to and reconnect with your writing, I predict that you will make incredible strides this year. The selection committee and I welcome you to composition at Cal Poly!

Dr. Brenda M. Helmbrecht
Director of Writing

Fresh Voices
Composition at Cal Poly

What to Expect in Your "Writing and Rhetoric" Course

Transitioning from High School English to College Writing

You will likely see some overlap between the classes you took in high school and the composition classes you will take at Cal Poly. This is by design. English 133 and 134 are not intended to be complete departures from your high school courses. Rather, your college writing courses offer you an opportunity to build on the skills you have been developing for the past few years. You will be asked to complicate and challenge the ways you already think about writing.

However, please know that even while you will find some overlap in terms of course content, your composition instructor's expectations will be different, perhaps higher. In short, you will be held accountable for your rhetorical choices. Your instructor will assume that when you write, you are making informed choices and s/he will determine and assess for the effectiveness of those choices. In effect, you won't just be regarded as a student. You will be treated like a *writer*.

In this new role, you will be expected to assume heightened responsibilities. In other words, you will need to attend class regularly, meet deadlines, and complete all of your coursework. When in class, your instructor will assume that you will have something thoughtful and meaningful to contribute.

If you felt constricted in your high school English classes (sometimes timed-writing and high-stakes exams can dominate a course's focus), regard English 133 or 134 not as a class that you *have to take,* but as an opportunity to really improve your writing so you can successfully navigate the many writing projects (including the Graduation Writing Exam) you will encounter throughout your career at Cal Poly.

Perspectives
Photograph by Jon Bartel

Course Curriculum

While English 133/134 courses are shaped by our instructors' unique approaches to teaching writing, each section still tends to follow a parallel curriculum, thereby ensuring that each section meets the same learning objectives. While the papers you write in your course may not be exactly the same as the assignments described below, you will likely be writing papers that are comparable in purpose and approach.

Exploring Significant Moments

This essay is often written during the first week of the class—although some instructors require students to revisit and revise it again at the end of the quarter. In many of these essays, students reflect on their experiences as writers, drawing attention to the importance of developing a writing process, the challenges of writing, and the sense of accomplishment they experience after recognizing their development as writers. Other essays will explore a significant moment in the writer's life—an experience that helped shape him/her.

Please note that these essays go beyond just telling a story: they each have a discernible focus and a purpose. Ultimately, these students are assessing their own abilities and experiences. You may find yourself nodding in agreement as you read these essays because you may have had similar experiences in your own life. On the other hand, you may be unable to directly relate to a particular writer's narrative—but, as a reader, your role is to *find* ways to connect with these writers' experiences. As you read, use these points of similarity and difference to help you consider your own experiences.

Profiling a Person, Place, Event, or Trend

In each of the profile essays included in this volume of *Fresh Voices*, students carved out distinctive approaches to the assignment—approaches that permitted them to explore exceptional elements found in cultures surrounding them. Topics for the profile sequence vary by instructor; some instructors select a theme, such as the environment or media. Other instructors ask students to use this assignment to become better acquainted with an aspect of someone's life, a well-loved place, or even a social trend. For many instructors, conducting an effective interview—and learning how to accurately represent someone else's point of view—is an essential component of this essay.

You will find that this assignment challenges you to synthesize multiple texts and viewpoints: your analytic response to your interviewee's work, the interview itself, and, when appropriate, your own experiences and responses. If you choose to profile a place or a trend, you will also learn to incorporate field notes and other outside sources. In addition, you must account for and write to an audience that does not have knowledge of your essay's subject matter. In other words, you need to present your own "insider's perspective" about the profile subject. But remember: regardless of who or what you profile, this essay is created and shaped by you. In other words, your profile subject needs to speak *with* you as a writer, not *for* you.

Analysis

Learning how to analyze a text is one of the most important skills you will learn in English 133/134. Whether you are studying an advertisement or a speech, identifying the strategies an author/artist uses to persuade an audience helps you better understand how the argument is conveyed. In particular, your class will make a distinction between summary (what a text says) and analysis (how a text conveys its message). Breaking a text down to its individual parts helps you better understand how the text makes meaning for its readers.

Public Rhetoric and Argumentation

For this sequence, students choose a public issue and write a persuasive essay supporting their viewpoint on it. The persuasive essays in this collection cover a broad range of subjects. Yet you will see one common feature: the authors have a personal stake in their chosen topic—an important component that can bring energy to any persuasive essay.

So meta? No meta? Still hurts.
Photograph by Marya Figueroa

In writing your own Public Rhetoric essay, you will learn that a well-written and fully-supported argument requires you to conduct research both to support your own claims and to fairly depict opposing viewpoints. You will also learn to use the rhetorical appeals of *ethos*, *pathos*, and *logos* (defined below) to persuade and connect with your chosen audience. Regardless of the topic you choose, it's generally best to select a focus that matters to *you*, something you want to understand better. Better yet: select a topic you want to learn more about. Try not to approach your topic with a firmly held point-of-view; proving what you already *think* you know isn't the goal of this essay. Rather, as you conduct research and learn about your topic, your position may shift. Rhetorical inquiry and engagement requires this kind of flexibility.

Final Project

Each section of English 133/134 completes the course differently. Regardless of the kind of assignment you are given, it will require you to draw from everything you have been taught throughout the quarter. This assignment can be regarded as the capstone to the course.

Key Course Concepts

Rhetoric

In its most basic terms, rhetoric generally refers to written, verbal, and visual persuasion. While you may have studied rhetoric in your high school English class, you will approach this concept through many different angles in your college writing classes.

According to Aristotle, rhetoric is defined as the ability of "observing, in any given case, the available means of persuasion." In short, rhetoric refers to your ability to make effective choices when speaking and writing. Yet the word "observe" here is also key: it refers to your ability to look at how rhetoric is used *on* you, even when you are not consciously aware of it. With this definition in mind, you will study how rhetoricians—including you—persuade people to consider their point of view. Every time you sit down to write, you must account for the ways in which you want your audience to respond to your text. What means are available to you as you seek to persuade people to change their position on an issue? If you lose track of the rhetorical situation and forget to consider how to best communicate with and persuade your reader, your essay may not affect your readers the way you intend. In effect, every act of writing becomes an act of persuasion.

The Rhetorical Appeals

Throughout your ENGL 134 course, you will encounter three rhetorical concepts that may be new to you: *ethos*, *pathos*, and *logos*. We have borrowed these terms from Aristotle, who long ago argued that every writer who wants to communicate effectively with his or her audience must account for these appeals.

So when writing, keep these three concepts in mind:

Ethos: Credibility

When we use this term, we are simply talking about credibility. In other words, writers must develop a strong *ethos* for readers to regard the argument as credible. Audiences are most persuaded by writers who have the knowledge to write intelligently about a given subject, and audiences trust writers who present information accurately and fully. On the other hand, they tend not to trust writers who leave out relevant information or who don't work with reliable sources. For instance, if a writer continually relies on web pages with no clear authors or publication dates (including Wikipedia), the argument may not be convincing. However, if a writer uses sources that have a track record of presenting information without a great deal of bias and that promote writers who conduct trustworthy research, the writer's own *ethos* is increased and the audience is more likely to be persuaded.

Ethos can also be developed when writers simply share a relevant personal experience that gives them insider knowledge. So if you want to write an essay about water politics and your family owns a farm that struggles to obtain an adequate amount of water, it would make sense to share that information in your essay in order to build credibility as a writer. There are many ways to develop your *ethos*—some of them quite subtle. You will study these approaches in your course.

Pathos: Emotion

Readers are most invested in and persuaded by ideas to which they have a deep emotional connection. Even Aristotle, who believed rhetoric shouldn't rely on manipulating readers' emotions in order to persuade them, still conceded that a rhetorician will only be effective if he can garner some emotional response from the audience. Effective rhetorical moments, then, touch the reader on a deeper, emotional level. But the question is, *how* do you want the readers to feel? Moreover, how do you get a reader to feel as intensely about a subject as you do? In order to ensure that readers share your emotions when reading your work, you must first attempt to predict the elements that will encourage your readers to engage with your writing on an empathic or sympathetic level. When writing, you must account for your readers' beliefs, values, and other personal attributes that they respond to emotionally. Do you want them to feel anger? Frustration? Sadness? Joy? Do you want them to feel motivated to go out into the world and make changes? When deciding which words best convey your ideas, keep in mind the emotional impact of language.

As a reader, you must also develop a critical awareness that enables you to determine if an argument overuses *pathos*. In other words, if an argument relies on your emotive response to persuade you and forgoes any other means of persuasion, you should be suspicious of it. The key here is balance. There is a fine line between persuasion and manipulation, but it's a distinction that every skilled rhetorician must make.

Logos: Reason

Though a piece of writing must make some use of *pathos*, emotions must still be balanced with logic. *Logos* refers to the entire structure of an argument. Does the argument overall make rational sense? Have you selected the kinds of sources that will encourage your reader to be persuaded by the logic of the argument? Perhaps you will want to look at scientific studies. Perhaps you can find some useful statistics to back up your ideas. Look for smaller ways to build a logical argument. For instance, using language like, "everyone knows…" automatically forces the reader to question your logic. After all, is there anything that "everyone knows"? Can you really account for everyone? As you conduct research and structure your essays, keep in mind that audiences like to see information presented rationally and logically.

Using the Three Appeals

You will learn that every effective paper has *ethos, pathos,* and, *logos* coursing through it. However, some arguments—depending on their subject and purpose—may require that one appeal be stronger than the other two. For instance, if you are writing an argument about a highly technical subject, you may find yourself relying on *logos* more than *pathos*. Conversely, you can also find support for an argument that relies on all three appeals equally. For instance, you may find a statistic about the harm done to the marine life in the recent Gulf Oil Spill. This one bit of evidence approaches the topic logically (*logos*), makes your reader feel both angry and sad (*pathos*), and, because the evidence is from a trustworthy, independent source, heightens your credibility (*ethos*).

You will be able to use these appeals more effectively if you keep in mind the entire rhetorical situation, which can often be represented by **Aristotle's rhetorical triangle:**

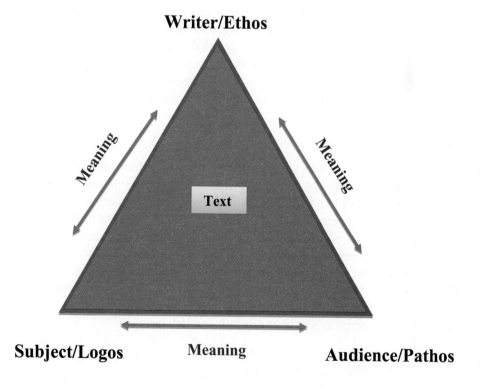

Writer/Ethos

Meaning

Meaning

Text

Subject/Logos   Meaning   **Audience/Pathos**

As you can see, the arrows here represent meaning. In other words, the rhetorical triangle tells us that a writer must account for the ways in which meaning moves back and forth between the three points—the writer, the subject, and the audience—simultaneously. Moreover, note that each arrow moves in two directions, indicating that that meaning also moves in multiple directions (not just one direction). In other words, the audience you are writing for should influence how you present the subject, and both of those elements should influence your *ethos*. As you write, let these triadic relationships shape your text. After all, if you forget about your audience as you write and only focus on your subject and your *ethos,* your meaning will not be communicated in the way you intend.

Making Effective Rhetorical and Stylistic Choices

Too often, we think about writing only in terms of correctness. We become consumed with what's right and what's wrong and we forget that, as writers, we have control over our own writing choices. While there will certainly be an emphasis on grammar and mechanics in your composition course, you may be asked to think about these concepts through a stylistic lens.

"Style" can be regarded as a rhetorical concept that is less about error and more about the choices you make as a writer. In other words, you can make stylistic choices that break the rules. Yet, you must first understand the rules, and you need to account for how the choices you make affect the text and the reader (consult the rhetorical triangle above). For instance, we know that a fragment is not a complete sentence and that we generally need to write with complete sentences. But what if, for once, you don't want a complete sentence. Just a fragment. Is that okay?

Or what if you want to use "I"? Or you directly want to address the reader with "you"? What if you want a one-sentence paragraph? Or what if you want to stop relying on commas and periods and instead want to try semicolons, colons, and dashes?

As you develop your writing style, work to make conscious, deliberate choices. Style is something writers work at; it's not innate. If a reader asks why you used that fragment, you need to be able to explain what effect you wanted that fragment to have. You will make good choices and some that are a little shaky—but that's okay. Style takes practice and, perhaps even more importantly, it requires you to take some risks with your writing. Sometimes the safest choice isn't the best one. So turn off the grammar check and start making your own decisions!

Conducting an Interview

The key to conducting a good interview is to devise questions that enable you to capture your interviewee's candor and insights as fully as possible. As the interviewer, you are not the star of the interview; rather, think of the interview in terms of collaboration and discussion. Try to meet with your subject in a setting that can reveal something about her profession, past-times, or beliefs. You can set the tone for the interview by asking important questions when your subject is laughing, smiling genuinely, and just seems relaxed—moments when she is comfortable discussing tricky subjects. While uncompromising and unflinching questions can make for a dramatic essay, you still have a responsibility to approach your interviewee respectfully. Ideally, after the interview begins, get out of your subject's way and let her take hold of the interview by offering thoughtful responses to your carefully crafted questions.

How to Write Interview Questions

Writing questions for an interview can be tricky. Knowing which questions to ask and how to ask them makes all the difference. The following are five simple tips to help you write interview questions.

1. Avoid asking "double-barreled questions."

These questions actually hide multiple questions within them. For example the question, "Do you think he is telling the truth and that he deserves to be set free?" actually contains two questions. When asked double-barreled questions, the respondent will most likely just answer one of them and you may not get the information you seek. Thus, it's better to separate your questions.

2. Refrain from asking biased or leading questions.

Avoid asking questions that are slanted towards an opinion or viewpoint. A good interview question is neutral and allows the respondent to give his or her own take on an issue. Your question should not influence the respondent's opinion.

3. Avoid questions that assume a specific response.

Some questions have already assigned opinions to the interviewees. Note this question preceded by a statement: "A lot of people are angered by this crime. Are you one of them?" This question is structured in such a way that an issue is painted as a crime when it probably still needs to be proven. You can secure this same information by simply asking, "Do you believe a crime took place?"

4. Keep your questions short and clear.

Sometimes brevity is key. Long, detailed questions may confuse your subject and you may not get a detailed response in return. Write questions that are short and concise. The stylistic choices you make are essential, too; the slightest grammatical or punctuation mistake can change a question's meaning.

5. Ask questions beginning with WHY, HOW, WHAT, and WHEN.

Your interview won't actually reveal much information if you rely on questions that elicit "yes" or "no" as a response. Devise open-ended questions to which you don't know the answer. Give your subject space to think carefully and thoughtfully about a question. And be prepared to go off-script and ask follow-up questions if you want to know more about your subject's responses.

Writing with Images

"Pictures are supposed to be worth a thousand words. But a picture unaccompanied by words may not mean anything at all. Do pictures provide evidence? And if so, evidence of what? And, of course, the underlying question: do they tell the truth? [...] A captionless photograph, stripped of all context, is virtually meaningless. I need to know more."

Errol Morris, Documentary Filmmaker
"Liar, Liar, Pants on Fire," The New York Times

As members of a visual culture, we must learn how to navigate, interpret, and analyze the messages conveyed to us via imagery. Many English 133/134 instructors ask students to study images through a rhetorical lens, which means that students explore how images make rational arguments (*logos*), how they evoke an emotional response from a viewer (*pathos*), and how (when used effectively) images can enhance a writer's or speaker's credibility (*ethos*). In other words, instructors want students to analyze images to understand how they communicate with an audience.

LOOK HERE

To read Errol Morris's essay on the relationship between captions and images, click here: http://opinionator.blogs.nytimes.com/2007/07/10/pictures-are-supposed-to-be-worth-a-thousand-words/

Analyzing visual rhetoric allows us to understand both the explicit and implicit arguments that images make about culture and society. Many people wrongly regard the act of examining an image as an effortless process, assuming that only a casual, quick glance is required. The sheer pervasiveness of images seems to place them outside the reach of critical reflection and analysis. Writing, on the other hand, is often seen as requiring careful planning and decision making to become effective. However, visuals and writing have much in common: they are intricately bound as they seek to entertain, to educate, and to persuade. Better understanding this relationship will enable you to approach the images you encounter—in advertising, in films and television, on *YouTube* and *My Space*, and even in video games—with a greater critical eye.

Additionally, readers may not be persuaded by written arguments alone; thus, when an image is effectively paired with text, the reader may get a fuller understanding of an issue. As you read *Fresh Voices*, focus on the relationship between the images and the writing. How do the images you see enhance the written arguments? How do the visuals heighten appeals to *ethos*, *logos*, and *pathos*?

When reading the following photo essay, "SLO Street," written by Cal Poly student David Maxson in his English 134 course, note the relationship between the images and the captions. Is Errol Morris right? Are images without captions "meaningless"? After the photo essay, you will find an analytic essay wherein David explains the choices he made as he took photos and composed their captions.

SLO Streets

Thoughts concerning a town geared towards people, not machines

San Luis Obispo city planners intentionally created extra-wide sidewalks to encourage visitors and locals to walk instead of drive

On this lovely evening, a young family enjoys a stroll in downtown SLO

SLO's pedestrian-centered design gives the town a friendly, safe atmosphere

In fact, the city's design is one of the key factors in making SLO America's happiest city

Most other cities across America have narrow sidewalks and little or no accommodation for bicycles

These kinds of sidewalks discourage walking and biking, forcing community members to drive

Compare these hectic, car-dominated streets to the alley below; which would you prefer around your home? Where would you want your children playing?

Photo courtesy of Eric Kane from TreeHugger.com

We should beseech our officials to consider pedestrians, not just cars, when designing our cities

It can be difficult for a city to preserve this kind of beautiful landscape—so wherever you end up living, make sure that officials don't merely take care of machines: make sure they take care of the people

SLO Streets: Analysis

David Maxson

SLO Streets is meant to be subtly persuasive, seeding the pro-pedestrian idea into the minds of readers without feeling combative or immediate. The hope is that by implanting these ideas in a positive light and allowing the reader to consider the contrasts presented, the reader will convince himself that making cities pedestrian-friendly is worthy of his support to some degree or another in the future. Because of the costly nature of changing cities, no immediate action is demanded; instead, future development is encouraged. In short, the persuasive purpose is to invite readers to passively accept what is needed.

The photographic essay format lends itself to this kind of subtlety for at least two reasons. First, photos in and of themselves are appeals to emotion and rarely contribute to the logical argument of the piece. Second, they can present points drawn from the reader's own mind without demanding counter-arguments.

Photography is largely an appeal to pathos. If contained in a logical argument, this kind of appeal by itself could be considered a fallacy, and thus detract from the credibility of the author. With photography, however, it instead brings up emotions in the viewer that words could not conjure so quickly. Images do not technically make an argument. That said, the impression left by an image can last a lifetime. This is why corporate logos and video advertising are universal necessities for large corporations. The graphic allows viewers to instantly make associations with past memories and emotions. For an example of how fast this works, think of the Google logo. Your eyes skim over the graphic, and you automatically know what it is referring to. Perhaps your first thoughts are about a big company; perhaps you think about finding information; whatever you individually use Google for, that's what comes to mind.

But that's not the only effect of the speed of images. Think again: though you cannot see the logo, can you remember the colors of each of the letters? Maybe you remember that the G is blue, but is the next letter red or yellow? Are there any green letters? The image and its details are unimportant by themselves, but what the image represents can be considered relevant. This kind of visual ignorance can be used in photo essays to convey a larger idea than each photo contains individually. Crowds, happiness, freedom, beauty, love—these ideas can be portrayed in a moment using an image, whereas using only words would be weak in comparison.

In "SLO Streets," the photos often have a single theme. The two most common shots are crowd and street photos. The crowds portray a certain systematic organization; the streets are portrayals of barrenness. Empty, painted streets feel inhuman and void. Crowded traffic is used to make the reader feel busy and cramped. The natural draw is back to the open lane where a father walks with his child, an image of peace. The reader does not even think to ask for a counter argument; and were he to want one, the writer could hardly give it. This is because no logical argument was really made. An appeal was made to the feeling and emotions of the reader, not to his logic.

This is the power of visuals, the subtlety of photography, and the emotion of images. If used properly, they can take the reader on a ride through his own imagination, and let him persuade himself there. He can take the complicated feeling of being compressed and show it perfectly with an image of traffic; he can induce tenderness by showing a baby, or a feeling of satisfaction by showing a young family smiling. This is how the crowds and traffic were used in "SLO Streets," not to stand on the defensive against the reader, but to let the reader stand on the defensive himself.

David Maxson is a Computer Science major.

Exploring Significant Moments

What moments have shaped you as a writer? As a person?

Peruvian Street Market (Puno, Peru)
Photograph by Brenda Helmbrecht

Being open to new experiences, beliefs, cultures, and ways of thinking is an essential component of college life. Your shifting perspective may also require you to think about and use language in new ways in order to fully "render" your experience to a listener or reader. If you were asked to describe the above photograph—which depicts a market in Peru—which elements would you highlight? How would you account for the vast array of colors, textures, fabrics, lighting, activity, and overall mood and tone of the image? How could you use language to *show* this image to your reader?

WRITER'S MEMO

This essay was written in response to a prompt requesting students discuss their relationship with writing. As you will see, I take this relationship quite seriously, and literally. For students less enthused with the world of writing, let me say that this is, whether you like it or not, a relationship you will have all your life so take this class as an opportunity to improve that relationship. Think of your relationship with writing as an arranged marriage that gets better with effort: you fold the laundry and writing takes out the trash. Speaking of trash . . . learn how to use your semi-colons! It's not hard and it will save you from looking like an idiot when you realize at age nineteen that semi-colons are not just elaborate commas with a dot above them. Maybe grammar should be included in your relationship with writing. So for what it's worth, try to enjoy the writing process and even get a little bit creative. Teachers don't want to read the same boring essay and surely it isn't much fun to write one.

On Going Long Term and Avoiding the Thanksgiving Turkey Drop

Liana Meffert

I have a love affair with English. I date metaphors on the sly. Metaphors are great because they allow you to draw a connection between two completely different things: I am watching the ink of my pen slither onto the page of this paper. I dot my I's like the quick strike of a fanged-bite. However, my words are not venomous. I love writing. I just related a snake to a pen and a piece of paper, where else can you do that?

There was a time back in high school when writing and I were "on the rocks," so to speak. We do not like to talk about it too much; it is kind of a sensitive subject. It really was not writing's fault. I realize this now. It was my teachers' and the people that told my teachers it was necessary to compose us in such a formulated manner. I understand the virtues of a literary essay and the importance of proper grammar and structure. However, I must also respect myself as a writer in a committed relationship with writing. Grammar and punctuation—when set inside these restricting lines- can dampen our relationship. Sometimes I need to linger on the important stuff . . . (and set aside the things I choose to forget).

I started writing poetry and going to coffee shops late at night. Sneaking out of the house after dark to nurture a seemingly forbidden love. Our relationship was bi-polar. By day, writing and I sat at desks, scrambling together for an A and neglecting our love. The sentence: "In (insert author here)'s book (*Italicize the title because that is MLA format*) . . . one can perceive . . . the presence of an omnipotent . . . (this is where I put together my favorite fancy words into a sentence I hope is cohesive enough to pass as an introduction). I was abusing writing. My heart was not in it and writing knew that. It hurt us both.

So in secret, I re-kindled my relationship with writing. At night we would slip away to spoken words *emanating enthusiasm*. I saw writing twist and turn in splendid new forms; it was a beautiful dance: we fell in love all over again. The words moved across the stage, twirling down the the microphone and into me. I watched lips so close they kissed it as they spoke. Sometimes mine almost kissed the microphone, too, like we were all united by an impassioned kiss of the same cause. That was relationship counseling for writing and me.

Even when the words were not mine, they were beautiful and I listened hard because someday (I knew if I listened hard enough) they could be mine. They would be mine. So I sipped coffee and warmed my face on steamy inspiration. Sometimes people would get up and say things that they could never say in real life. I loved thinking that somewhere along the way they had written down something because it felt real to them and it needed to be said. Now, the power of that paper and those written words propagated a confidence, ignited only by listening ears and hot stage lights. In some ways, if it has already been written down, it has already been said, and the re-telling of that story is never as scary as the initial draft.

LOOK HERE

Many writers develop a style and "voice" that is truly unique. David Foster Wallace is no exception. His 2005 commencement speech uses language and rhetorical techniques to connect with his readers in memorable ways. Read his speech here:
http://moreintelligentlife.com/story/david-foster-wallace-in-his-own-words

Needless to say, writing and I are on the mend. I hear a lot of relationships don't make it through college. But I think writing and I will be an exception. College seems a bit more respectful of our relationship. Sometimes, and here I will admit this written piece is a bit of an experiment, grammar does not allow for the correct expression of voice. When I write, I talk in my head just as the lips on microphones spoke to me all those nights. I replay that melodic, slow ooze of poetry. When I revise, I read out loud to myself. I pause, insert commas, read again. Maybe I do this because when I read books I am careful to pause (mentally) at all the appropriate places. If someone were to read my writing it just seems like common courtesy to provide him or her with the same instructions. Instead of punctuation as a matter of formality, I think of it as set of directions: this is how I want you to read my writing.

I am thinking of e.e. Cummings. That was not much of an introductory sentence, but this is not high school. I appreciate more than anything his use of parenthesis. I also liked the placement of words and phrases. Writing has never looked so versatile. Like providing a set of instructions for reading, but also a map with each word in its own location to be considered at the appropriate place in time.

I was dangerously close to going on a tangent; this could cloud the "clear purpose" of the essay, which seems to be one of the only rules to college writing and rhetoric. The clear purpose was to reveal my love of writing whilst simultaneously trying not to sound like I was sucking up to my English teacher. I will add that I am only revealing our relationship for the purpose of this piece. Usually writing and I date in quiet over coffee or between sheets (of paper).

Liana Meffert is a psychology major.

CONSIDER THIS

- *Meffert describes punctuation as a "set of directions" indicating "how I want you to read my writing." In effect, she offers a more complex way to think about grammar and punctuation than just a set of rules that dictate what's right and what's wrong in an essay. Take another look at her essay. Note the moments when her punctuation—including ellipses, semicolons, parenthesis, and dashes—compel her reader to interact with her sentences in very specific, deliberate ways.*
- *This essay relies on metaphor to describe Meffert's history as a writer. Can you create a metaphor that best explains your own relationship with writing?*

WRITER'S MEMO

The Writer's History assignment was my favorite assignment from English 134. I hadn't pondered how my writing had evolved from its early stages into what it is today prior to this assignment. I realized that as I attempted to explain my maturation as a writer, I could not help but notice that I only grew as a writer once I had abandoned the notion that a composition can only be effective when written in a certain way. In "From Constraint to Freedom," I took what I perceived to be a risk at the time and contrasted writing with math in order to allow the reader to see inside my mind as my writing developed. This essay was written in response to a prompt requesting students discuss their relationship with writing. As you will see, I take this relationship quite seriously, and literally. For students less enthused with the world of writing, let me say that this is, whether you like it or not, a relationship you will have all your life so take this class as an opportunity to improve that relationship. Think of your relationship with writing as an arranged marriage that gets better with effort: you fold the laundry and writing takes out the trash. Speaking of trash . . . learn how to use your semi-colons! It's not hard and it will save you from looking like an idiot when you realize at age nineteen that semi-colons are not just elaborate commas with a dot above them. Maybe grammar should be included in your relationship with writing. So for what it's worth, try to enjoy the writing process and even get a little bit creative. Teachers don't want to read the same boring essay and surely it isn't much fun to write one.

From Constraint to Freedom

George Rodriguez

When I look back on the moment when I was first taught how to write correctly, I remember feeling as though writing and mathematics were one in the same. As a young elementary school student, my paradigm of what writing actually was had been molded into the same cookie-cutter shape as every other kid in my class. I was forced to structure paragraphs in specific ways and use introductory language that inevitably made my writing feel like a clumsy hodgepodge of structured sentences. Paragraphs became math problems that only required the writer to put in each component and arrive at a definite, singular answer.

I recall the first time I was introduced to "the paragraph" in the third grade. I do not recall my teacher ever going over how to structure a paragraph, but I do remember coming home and asking my father how to write a paragraph. He explained to me that a paragraph starts with a topic sentence and ends with a concluding sentence. Secondly, he pointed out that each sentence in between should have an introductory word such as "first" or "also," followed by a comma. My first inclination was to relate writing to the rigidity of a math problem. I began to tell myself that each and every paragraph must have the same structure and that my only job was to fill in the gaps between the topic sentence, introductory words and concluding sentence. Looking back now, I see how my dad's writing advice was sufficient for what my teacher wanted to see in a third grader's writing.

LOOK HERE

The relationship between STEM fields and the Humanities is rather complex. For a current perspective on how the disciplines need to support each other, read Paul Jay and Gerald Graff's editorial "Fear of Being Useful":
http://www.insidehighered.com/views/2012/01/05/essay-new-approach-defend-value-humanities

My paragraphs constructed of pre-shaped puzzle pieces were well liked by my teachers at the time and this only reinforced my newly found flawed form of writing. Despite this, I could not help but feel that there was something missing in my writing. Prior to being introduced to paragraph writing, I had enjoyed the adventures of writing without boundaries or adherence to any rules. I can remember the feeling of being constrained in my writing. There were details that I had to share with the world, even at a young age, but they were unable to shine behind the clouds of paragraph writing. I felt as though I had been crippled by the structure of composition and was beginning to feel my interest progressively drift from writing the more that I wrote; similar to two like-charged magnets brought in close proximity to one another. As the magnets move closer, the repulsive force becomes greater and greater. Each writing assignment furthered my apathy for writing that I would not shake for quite some time.

My writing career, up to my sophomore year, is mostly a blur. I would bet that this is largely due to the fact that my compositions and writing prompts were mundane and dry. They lacked edgy, critical analysis and were merely statements of fact or summarizations. I myself even understood that my writing was somewhat mind-numbing, but my papers received A's and that was all that mattered to me. As a sophomore I decided I was done composing lame papers and I enrolled in Honors English. I did not know what to expect, having never been in an advanced English class. In our first essay we were given the task of rejecting, defending, or qualifying a profound quote out of Mary Shelley's *Frankenstein*. In my head I proclaimed, "We have choices!?" I was astonished that we were given the freedom to dictate the journey our paper took our reader on.

Our instructor, Mr. Hayden, enthusiastically emphasized how much he wanted to read papers with critical analysis of the quote. He did this all while brandishing his hands vigorously and with drastic fluctuations in his voice, as only a trained competition debate and dramatic interpretation instructor could do. He encouraged us to vary the syntactical structures we used in our essays; to start with gerunds, to use inverted syntax, to use a fragment for emphasis.

With my newly acquired freedom, I took on this new venture. As I completed this assignment, I realized that when given the freedom to allow my analysis to flow wherever it needed to in order to arrive at its final destination, I did not despise writing. Thankfully, I was not limited to certain pieces to use in my writing and I had choices that I could make. Language and composition are a way of interpreting the world around us just as much as math and science. Greek philosophers such as Aristotle and Plato did not have the mathematics to explain the processes they saw in the world. They had to look to language to decipher the universe as they saw it. I am fascinated with the idea that language itself is ambiguous and each individual perceives different words and combinations of words in a unique way. Writing is about capturing that ambiguity and controlling it in a way that will allow the reader room to ponder, yet allows the author to instill their purpose into the reader through personal diction and connotation. I agree with the maxim that perception is reality. What an individual writes will influence the reader's perception, but each reader will be taken into a different world based on their own experience.

My writing journey has brought me to a place where I enjoy the intricacies of language and rhetoric and I owe this largely to Mr. Hayden. From the rigid structuring of a paragraph to the passionate writing instruction from Mr. Hayden, it has been a long journey to where I am today. I believe that I am a much better writer today than I was before my sophomore year. My intrigue in diction that I discovered within myself is what drives my writing and I pride myself on being as accurate as possible with each word I choose. Gone are the days of writing as though I were setting up a math problem. Now the only similitude I see between writing and math is that both seek to explain the world that we, as human beings, perceive.

George Rodriguez is a mechanical engineering major.

CONSIDER THIS

- *In every piece of writing there is an inextricable link between its form and its content. A writer's stylistic choices shape the form an essay takes and can simultaneously color its content. In the second paragraph of this essay, Rodriguez seems to be utilizing the relationship between form and content in a very specific way. Can you describe how he is using form to convey his meaning in that paragraph? Look at his word choices and his paragraph structure. How do these choices work to support his thesis?*
- *Rodriquez states, "language itself is ambiguous and each individual perceives different words and combinations of words in a unique way." Why might you consider this statement to be true? Could this statement be challenged? How?*

WRITER'S MEMO

Writing papers in college is an interesting experience. There are no pre-set formulas or teacher mandated "plug and play" templates that students must follow and use to get a good grade. Due to a lack of hard and fast guidelines, college students are able to create their own unique writing style and take a variety of approaches to tackle multiple writing situations. Although, I cannot help any of you find your inner writer (it is up to you to discover it), I can impart two tips that can help you in your writing. The first tip is to always start as early as possible—preferably two to four weeks in advance—since it allows time to brainstorm ideas, to draft, and [time]for multiple revisions. Also, you will be able to balance your college lifestyle at Cal Poly because you will be smothered with work in the latter part of the ten-week quarter. The second tip is revising your essays (multiple times) with particular focus on conciseness, the overall logical flow of an essay, and your individual writing problems. By doing this, you are making your papers more coherent and appealing to readers which can help better transmit your ideas (this is what writing is about) and perhaps improve your grade (if that is your goal). By using these two tips, you can improve your writing and succeed in college.

The Writing Revolution

Anthony Wong

Many have watched the movie *The Matrix*, but I have lived in it for eighteen years. During my imprisonment, I was constantly programmed with the machines' logic and views, and if there was any defiance, I would be ruthlessly punished by the Matrix's agents. I know most of you who are reading this either think I am delusional or that I really had a cool life that involved saving the world and humanity from the clutches of the machines. Sadly, my life story isn't really exciting, in fact, it is really mundane, but I did live in the Matrix, just not the one that you are all familiar with.

I was plugged inside the Matrix known as the "K–12" for eighteen years. During my imprisonment, the agents of writing—Ms. Ford, Ms. Tripepi, and Ms. Williams—radically changed me as a writer. As optimistic as this sounds, it really isn't because these agents took away my writing life and replaced it with the "standard" program of writing. They constantly ingrained my mind with how to write a "perfect" five paragraph essay and how to write a "proper" paragraph with one concrete detail and two commentaries. This model severely crippled my ability to write. For hours, until my brain turned to mush, I would be pacing around my room trying to think of the "perfect" essay that would fulfill all the expectations of my agent. I would just sit there with a well-gnawed pencil and a desk overflowed with "failed" papers. Eventually, I would find something inspiring to write about, but it would usually become a "failed" paper. After being frustrated by such a simple assignment, I would say "screw it" and start writing just to get that assignment out of the way. Every time I did this, my agent will reward me with an "A" for the length of my essay instead of judging its content. After passing all of my English classes, my agents thought they had taught me to write, but no, that was not true. I didn't learn how to write, but I did learn how to bullshit all my writing assignments.

I know there are some of you who can sympathize with me on this issue and others who wonder why I didn't just pursue my own creativity instead of just writing what they wanted. I would like to let you know that I did occasionally try to be creative, but that didn't help me "pass." Every time I would try to submit a creative paper, it will always be returned to me with blood streaking down it skin, barely alive, and stripped of its soul. This is the outcome experienced by all my papers that didn't meet their set standard. After receiving my paper back, I would pull my hair and scream out in anguish at the agents. This would continue to repeat until my senior year of high school where I met the teacher that pulled me out of the abyss of formulaic writing and back into the realm of creative writing.

LOOK HERE

For more information about voice and tone in writing, follow this link to the "Grammar Girl" website: http://grammar.quickanddirtytips.com/understanding-voice-and-tone-in-writing.aspx

During my last year at high school, I met Mr. Ireland, one of the most amazing English teachers that I have ever had. Unlike the agents of the system, Mr. Ireland did not care for the formulaic approach and encouraged me to write with my own style. He fought to unplug me from the system that had taken control of me. Unfortunately, after years of being brainwashed by the agents, I no longer remembered how to write with my own style.

For months, I struggled to define my own sense of style as a writer. A style that did not include the agents' formula, no, my style would be like a river winding and twisting around obstacles, able to adapt to any situations. I was finally able to tap into this style under the tutelage of Mr. Ireland. Like Morpheus saving Neo by showing him the real world, Mr. Ireland finally unplugged me from the system by simulating a college environment for me in Advanced Placement Literature. There were no rules and formulas in his class; there was only my pen, my ideas, and my own style of writing. In addition to the large degree of freedom, I was shown how to use techniques like iambic pentameter, enjambments, allusions, metaphors, and how to analysis symbols in poetry and literature like Fyodor Dostoyevsky's *Crime and Punishment* and Thomas Hardy's *Tess of the d'Urbervilles*, but the most important thing Mr. Ireland made me do was write and write. That was what finally freed me; I was free to write and I was treated like a college student when I wrote. There was an extremely high standard that I was held to and at first, I did not like it, but eventually I took up the challenge and started to write in my own voice and not just regurgitated what my agents wanted. That was how Mr. Ireland freed me from the Matrix.

After years of tearing my hair out and hitting my head against a wall, I began to rediscover my style as a writer, but more importantly I discovered what standards were expected of me in college. As I enter Cal Poly SLO, I want to build on the level of excellence that I received from Mr. Ireland and to infuse my writing with my own soul and words that will eventually create my identity as a writer.

Anthony Wong is a political science major

CONSIDER THIS

- *Wong parallels his writing experience with the plot of* The Matrix. *How does this comparison help his readers relate to his experiences? Does he account for readers who may not have seen the movie?*
- *How would you describe Wong's tone in his essay? How can a writer's tone affect readers and convey meaning more effectively?*
- *Wong believes the five-paragraph essay "severely crippled my ability to write." Can you recall a time when you felt constrained as a writer because of a formula?*

My Life, My Story, My Adventure

Alex Vice

My name was Leif, son of the blacksmith. To my left was Barda, the ex-captain of the royal guard before the kingdom was overthrown by the shadow. Behind us was Jasmine, the wild girl we found in the forest. Together we were destined to save the land that we loved by collecting the seven gems of the Belt of Deltora and finding the heir to . . . "SMACK!" the sound of the ruler resonating around a silent room of wide-eyed 10-year-olds was enough to make the most dastardly villain cringe. "Alex, since you seemed to be paying attention, why don't you repeat to the class the requirements for tonight's journal assignment." That was a typical day for me in class, it didn't matter what teacher I had back then either. I would sit at my desk and lose myself in the stories of those books I had read, I became the hero, I saved the world, and I got the girl. As for my teachers, the older I got the less they seemed to care that I wasn't paying attention. I suppose it took a few big events in my life for me to realize that writing has just as many benefits as reading does.

Before all else I was a reader. Not just any reader either, I was the best damned reader in the 4th grade at Placer Elementary School. Back in the day, reading was all I had. I wasn't a miniature sports prodigy like some of those kids. Hell, I didn't even do my homework back then, so grades certainly weren't in my favor. In fact, I was failing most of my subjects as a 4th grader! Well actually to clarify things, I probably wasn't the best reader either, but I did read more books than half the kids in our class-combined. That is something I will always be proud of. Anyways, I don't need to go into detail of how Mrs. Clark, my 4th grade teacher, was a horrid, she-devil, hell-bent on world domination. No, I'm pretty sure that I definitely don't need to expand on how I was the only one who saw through her evil charade, and that my attempts to foil her schemes always resulted in trips to the Emperor of Doom himself. Principal Cushinberry.

Don't let his name fool you; his favorite thing to do was force young adventurers, such as yours truly, to write apology letters to their teachers for not paying attention in class, or for "breaking school property." That was my first real exposure to writing. Those apology letters that explained how "sorry" I was, and how I "would never do that again." But you heard it from me first, that window had internal flaws. A scrawny 10-year-old could have never broken one without help.

There is a different window that I have only just recently started looking through though. Maybe this is just a lame cliché about some window metaphor, but it took a certain someone to show me that this window existed. Not long ago, I was staying the night at my grandparents while my parents were vacationing for their anniversary. It was a Saturday night and I was stuck with my grandparents and younger brother while my friends were, in my eyes, having the best time in their whole entire lives . . . without me.

Suffice to say, I was bored. I guess my grandpa noticed (maybe it was because I was beating up my brother for the umpteenth time that day) but he approached me with a big grin. I noticed he was holding his hands behind his back, as if to hide something. "Alex! I've got a surprise for you!" he said, in his usual way of yelling a few words, and then pausing before finishing his thought. Then, as he whipped his hand out from behind his back, I saw it. He held a small paperback book, the cover picture showing a dashing young man in a white tux pulling a beautiful lady in elegant blue gown behind him. I noticed they were running away from what seemed to be Middle Eastern Terrorists.

He was pointing with one finger to the title, *Dyed for Death*, and with another to the printed name of the author: Rick Rider. The only Rick Rider I knew happened to be the shaky old geezer standing in front of me! A hundred thoughts were racing through my head. I mean, I knew he had been an engineer in the Air Force; in fact, the man was a real life rocket scientist for crying out loud. I had a feeling that tiny little book would be my window into finding out more about the man behind all those awe inspiring, yet daunting, prestigious titles.

"Look! Who's that?!" His words suddenly snapped me out of my thoughts.

"Grandpa, is that you?"

"Yes sir!" his head was bobbing so violently, I thought for sure it would fall off!

"Wow Grandpa, can I read it?" I quickly asked to get him to calm down. To tell the truth I don't remember the rest of the conversation, because I was way too interested in reading that book.

The book wasn't very long as far as my standards go; however, it was a book I will never forget. Not because of the normal things we praise books for, it certainly wasn't a bestseller. No, I will always remember this book because it opened a small window for me into my grandpa's life. It didn't exactly tell me any truths about his life, but it did share with me some insight into his thoughts, his fears, and even his passions at the time he wrote it in the late 70s.

LOOK HERE

Since the Iranian Revolution of the late 1970s, Iran has recently experienced another wave of revolution following the presidential election in 2009. View a photo essay, published by the Boston Globe, *which documents the struggle and strife of the region's uprising:*
http://www.boston.com/bigpicture/2009/06/irans_disputed_election.html

What my grandpa really gave me was a sense of clarity and a goal. Maybe it's been a bit selfish of me to have read all of those books without giving anything back. I realized that obviously someone had to have written all those books I love, so maybe writing isn't all bad. Not that I won't have to overcome a few challenges before I get to that point though, mainly impatience. For example: how come my thoughts don't write themselves down? This is taking forever!

Now perhaps you could say that the adventures of a young man, caught up in the middle of the Iranian Revolution of the 1970s, mirrors some of the major points of my career maturing as a reader and into a prospective writer. But you couldn't possibly be able to make that connection, could you? Too bad there isn't a book out there with all that glorious information in it, just waiting for you to explore.

Alex Vice is a physics major.

CONSIDER THIS

- *Some of the key components which can be used to render a vivid memoir include: narrative voice, character description, setting, and dialogue. How do these elements help develop this memoir?*
- *In his title, Vice essentially promises to take his reader through an "adventure." Do you think he delivered on this promise? Did the title meet your expectations as a reader?*

WRITER'S MEMO

Writing this essay was really easy for me since the event I wrote about happened only last year. Everything was still pretty clear in my mind. After going through a few solid days of writing, a couple containers of Nutella and Oreos, and numerous revisions, I thought I produced a pretty good representation of how I felt about the event. I'd say picking an event that you can still vividly remember and staying off Facebook are two of the best things to consider when writing a personal narrative.

From Spandex to Soufflés

Jeffrey Shen

There is nothing I dread and loathe more beforehand but relish afterwards than racing my bike. As I slowly roll my way up to the line, I recall the first race of the season where I was forced to race in the midst of an illness, coughing and hacking my way to sixth place. Now sixth place may not seem like a bad result for a league that encompasses students from all over California, but when the podium only goes five deep, it is the last place I want to be. Today is the day I redeem myself.

Arriving at the line my stomach churns violently as if the goldfish I swallowed freshman year somehow lay dormant all this time and is now thrashing his way out. Ahead of us stands a man bearing a clipboard and cheap headpiece that leads to a bulky megaphone sagging at the side of his waist. "Racers. . . ." He begins to brief the anxious teenagers about racing etiquette, though it is apparent that his monotone voice proves to be no match for the sea of cowbells and screaming teammates. "3. 2. 1. Be safe have fun." With those words the bystanders are swept up in a whirlwind that can only be created by a sprinting pack of cyclist. Heavy breathing surrounds me as I mash my way through a labyrinth of spandex. My scratchy throat throbs with every gasp of air, as if I am drinking a cup of glass shards; my lungs on fire. Luckily, the twisty dirt trail begins to give way to a mellow road as the first lap is coming to an end, giving me a chance to get a drink. The smooth tarmac offers unparalleled relief; coasting, I reach down for my bottle and start to bring the cool elixir to my lips. My sandpapery tongue anticipates the slightly sweet,

creamy orange sports drink I prepared the previous night. Before the nectar can grace my lips, I faintly hear the buzzing of two tires touching. NO, I think to myself, but it is too late. Blurry images of my bike, the pavement and sky swirl into one form as if God has put the earth in a washing machine. I try to get up from the ground and remount my bike, but I can't. Something feels weird. I instantly reach for my left collarbone. It feels like someone filled a balloon up with rocks. No-no-no-no-no. I start yelling: no words, just pure noise. Racers continue to swoosh around me, some looking at me more than others, but all leaving me helplessly in the road.

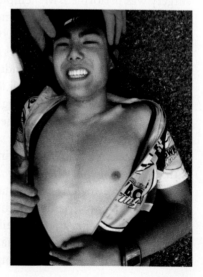

EMTs arrive immediately, which in adrenaline time seems like two hours. I do my best to stay composed, compensating the pandemonium building up inside. "I broke my collarbone. I have done this before. I'm fine, I can get up. Where's my bike?" My ignorant self-assessment proves to be underwhelming, as they continue to hold me down, unzipping my jersey. One of the ladies pulls out her iPhone and takes a picture of me, "You see this? We can't let you get up, we're calling an ambulance." I faintly notice myself on the screen trying to smile, flashing an insincere thumbs-up. The masquerade quickly deteriorates though as my eyes moves toward a white protrusion on my shoulder. Wait, did she say ambulance? I quickly protest the ten thousand dollar ride to no avail as the EMT in the background nods her head as she confirms the location of the race venue by phone.

LOOK HERE

Take a free bike safety and skills course with the San Luis Obispo Bike Coalition: www.slobikelane.org Learn more about riding safely in traffic with Road ID's "Rules of The Road" videos: www.roadid.com/roadrules/

"Want some morphine?" the young paramedic asks, "We're gonna drive through some road construction. Better be ready for a bumpy ride." I take some. The pothole riddled road seems slightly less painful compared to the torment I begin to experience as I realize that my racing season may be over. I frantically ask the laid-back paramedic about the timeline of recovery for my injury. An IV bag sways back and forth above me as if it is the pendulum of a grandfather clock, mocking my vulnerability against time. It's obvious I will not be able to ride a bike this season, let alone do anything involving motion. Seeing my body tense with anguish, the paramedic chimes in, "Hey, if you're lucky this ambulance might go to Davis. There are some pretty hot nurses in the hospital at UC Davis. Just depends what is closer." I just nod, as the ambulance continues on route to Sutter Roseville Medical Center.

It has been seven days since I last took a shower. Seven days since I was able to get up from my bed on my own. Seven days since I lost my sanity. Here I lie on my bed, arms to my side, legs straight and grimace overtaking my face. This position proves to be my only means of comfort, but in reality it is the most painful way to reside. Dust, that was once brown, peppers my skin into a black shade. Sweat from the race still coats my skin, giving it a grimy texture that sticks to the bed sheets. The only clean area on my body is a fresh, puffy white gauze taped over my shoulder where surgery was performed. My temples throb with anxiety and grief. Limbs and neck are stiffened from idleness. The rage in my mind makes my face hot to the touch. Training was going so well I thought, smugly reflecting back on my training schedule: morning ride before school, evening ride after school. While classmates plan beach gatherings for the weekend, I map out bike routes. But now I'm going to lose that endurance. The abrupt stop in activity makes my body quiver with angst. The buildup up of energy is too much; I need to get out. I spot the little red bell on my night stand among the pill bottles. Sluggishly, I begin crawling my dirty fingers across the crisp sheets, slowly pulling my arm towards the bell. I feel helpless, pathetic and full of anxiety.

Today is my first day back in school since the accident. Sitting in the cheap plastic chair of the incandescent lit classroom brings about a familiar feeling of stability. Handouts accumulate with each passing period, forcing a classmate to carry them for me due to my inability to bear a backpack. Nevertheless, I am ecstatic to once again converse with all my peers. During lunch I intently listen to my friends, waiting for some spark, some remnant of their lives that I can join. Soon though I realize that the daily banter I was once a part of now exemplifies my weakened state. The conversation slowly changes to the workout for today's mountain bike practice. Not being able to ride was worse enough, but the fact all my friends do after-school sports leaves me with yet another evening of seclusion. Lacking ambition, I slouch at my desk during fifth period, dejected, wondering what I could do after school.

Being in a sling makes it difficult to find a safe activity that satisfies my active appetite. I shift my attention upon the sunlit window next to me, gazing upon the gentle mountains in the distance. I coarsely whisper to the surrounding handful of students, "Anyone want to hike with me after school?" Of course, almost everyone quickly apologizes as they decline: listing the activities or practices they need to attend. Almost everyone that is, except Sarah. The quiet, floral–dressed girl hides two seats behind me. She ran cross country as a freshman with me, until her flat feet called it quits the following year. I know Sarah well enough to tell you that she doesn't talk in class unless spoken to, but if you wanted to know anything else, you're out of luck. Anyways, class is almost over and the goldfish in my stomach begins to slowly swim in circles as I anticipate my arrangement after school.

Sitting in the dirt parking lot outside the gated trails, I wait for Sarah. I begin reading my latest issue of *Mountain Bike Action* to pass the time but am unable to finish a single story. I look up from my reading with every passing car, hoping to see the dark green Corolla. Soon she rolls by, a plume of dust trailing her car. We start the walk with trivial talk about school work. The conversation soon segues into a sympathetic session, exchanging similar stories of suffering from sport inhibiting injuries. Cresting the top of the hill, my legs begin to ache from the sudden exposure to exercise, my tummy growling. Fantasizing, I tell her about a grilled portabella mushroom sandwich I made the other day. Before I could even describe it, Sarah chimes in, "Ooo, did you put roasted red bell peppers on it? Was it served on focaccia bread? Any caramelized onions?" I am smitten. Food has always been my passion, but since cycling engulfed my life I haven't had the opportunity to let that passion grow, let alone meet another foodie.

Three hours later, Sarah and I are buttering ramekins in my kitchen. Flour is being measured, chocolate tempered, and eggs separated. I stand next to the counter with one arm in sling and begin whisking the bowl of egg whites. My forearm burns and grows sore as I rhythmically beat the frothy mixture. I glance up at Sarah who is watching me. Before I can object, she takes the whisk from my hand and continues down the road to stiff peaks. Relieved, the throbbing in my arm subdues as I relax my hand from its earlier tightened grip. Standing back from the counter and absorbing the moment, a smile spreads over my face. A new assurance floods my veins, calmness envelops my body. There is nothing I would rather be doing right now. Biking was the problem, cooking is my elixir.

Jeffrey Shen is a biology major.

CONSIDER THIS

- *Shen takes readers through the moments after his injury. How would you characterize his tone from beginning to end? Does the tone shift? If so, how?*
- *The writer uses food as a theme in both the beginning and the end of the essay. How do his descriptions of food change? What does this shift tell the reader about Shen? What other themes does the writer use in his narrative?*
- *What strategies (verb tense, images, details) does the writer use to bring the reader into the narrative? Are there any specific descriptive or stylistic elements that stand out to you? How does Shen use these strategies throughout the essay?*

I Do This for Me

Danny Meritt

The dictionary definition of the word "hospital" reads: an institution in which sick or injured persons are given medical or surgical treatment. I spent ten days and over two hundred hours in the Lucia Packard Children's Hospital at Stanford University. I would later become one of the most remembered patients, not only because of my ridiculous height attempting to fit in a twin-sized bed, but because of the resulting complications of my experience. The surgery I endured opened my eyes to the realization of life's setbacks and the journey to success and self enlightenment through willingness and determination.

Rather than waking up to my usual black ihome chanting an annoying tune I cannot bear to listen to, I heard the constant beeping deriving from a heart beat monitor inches from my face. I scrounge around with my hands to see what constricts my arms, only to find three separate IV's propped outside my body like an octopus. With my only available movement I quickly swivel my head and spot a glimpse of various tubes sticking directly out of my chest. Surrounded by a prison of white curtains and empty chairs, a sign in the corner of my eye catches my attention, "Stanford Hospital". To my relief, a tall rather slim man strolls into the room in an all white suit and explains the situation and how I ended up in the nightmare.

Growing up, I had a rare chest deformity called Pectus Excavatum. Despite my luck, the majority of these cases include a slight depression of the sternum resulting in a "concaved" chest. In my particular situation, my sternum curved inward while also twisting similar to a corkscrew of a rollercoaster found at Six Flags. Until recently, I'd been oblivious to the resulting complications of the condition, which later tests revealed that my lungs were being constricted as a result of the irregular shaping of my bone. Other effects caused by the defect include scoliosis and inadvertently rounding of the shoulders creating a "hunchback" posture. Once these facts were revealed to me, the decision for surgery seemed imminent.

LOOK HERE

For more information on Pectus Excavatum and its symptoms, visit the Mayo Clinic's site dedicated to the subject.
http://www.mayoclinic.com/health/pectus-excavatum/DS01136

The doctor's voice seemed soothing to the immense pain endured with every move I made. Observing the tentacle tubes extending out of every corner of my body and the epidural sticking out of my spine, I found myself quickly in a panic. I immediately began filling my mind of possible scenarios of freak hospital accidents. Fortunately, a nurse walked in followed by my parents, and my nerves were quickly silenced. She explained that despite the elongated duration of the surgery, over two hours, the outcome was successful. Hearing these words I felt my heart and mind return to a semi-normal state.

Being deprived of eating any type of food for over twelve hours prior to my surgery did not sit well with my body. Immediately after hearing the sound of a food cart wheeled down the hall, my eyes stayed glued to the door waiting for the sweet smell of any nature of edible material. As a revered college as Stanford was, I imagined the food to be adequately fulfilling, possible prepared by a culinary arts major, or recognizable chef. Unfortunately, as the nurse lifted the tray cover, I quickly reminded myself that Stanford primarily focuses on doctors than cooks.

As every night came to a close, the nurse entered my chamber and commenced the nightly routine of explaining the fifty various pills I would be required to wake up and shove down my throat, thus guaranteeing absolutely no sleep. Yet before my first pill appointment, I was awoken by a constant "beep" blasting in my ear. The beep seemed similar to a remixed ihome but my conscious knew differently. I peered over my right shoulder and gazed onto a tiny screen, only to discover that whenever I cozily fell asleep, my oxygen level dipped below the standard human level, triggering an alarm. As a result the nurse required I shove two clear tubes up my nostrils to ensure the proper oxygen was delivered. These complications ripped apart my sanity, creating a closed cell where any feeling of departure seemed miles away.

Waking up in the morning I felt weaker than the day before; my arms ached from the constant flow of fluid through IV's and the inability to function my upper body. In addition to my excruciating pain, each day came equipped with challenges, ranging from seemingly simple to unthinkably impossible. The daily tests included sitting upward, with the help of my mom or a nurse, forcibly strutting to the bathroom with a feeling that my body was moments away from complete annihilation, and ultimately hiking to the end of the hall. With every test came a fail. With every fail brought a loss of hope. However, the thought of departing the presumably safe and comforting children's hospital, had never appeared so feasible until now.

Through the persistence of my friends and family pushing me to believe in myself, I conquered the daily tasks. Crossing these missions off my checklist, drew me one step closer to freedom. Each day brought new accomplishments including the removal of a tube or IV, a farther walk down the hall, and an improved knowledge of what not to order for dinner. Spending my days aimlessly staring at the walls, hoping for the day I would be released from this awful dream. In the morning my mother entered the room, which usually consists of asking her daily dose of twenty questions wondering how I slept? How the oxygen went? What had I ordered for breakfast? However, Sunday morning she entered without a single word except a tiny grin crossing her face almost too subtle to notice. Based off her expression, a warm sensation overcame my body and I realized that today is the day. The day I bid farewell to my second home, and give thanks to the nurses, doctors, and anesthesiologists who truly saved my life. As the thought sunk in deeper and deeper, my hands begun to shake, unfortunately with each movement my body endured severe soreness and pain. I gazed upon the room one last time, reminded of the accomplishments and improvements I made since the dreadful day of waking up. We packed up the car and engulfed myself in a human cocoon composed of various pillows and blankets to ensure that I had absolutely no movement whatsoever.

Pulling around the corner, smelling the fragrance of home, witnessing my family standing at the door, brought me to tears. Throughout the entire struggle and recovery, I had not shed one tear until arriving at the little brown structure called home. However, the perfect feeling of ecstasy soon dismissed as I realized my condition.

Over the next six months my body endured more rehab than I had previously known to exist. Many of the pains received during my exercises surpassed anything I suffered during my stay in the Hospital. Day in and day out I felt the urge to quit, giving up hope and realizing I would never return to my physical potential.

But I didn't. I worked my ass off swimming laps daily, lifting weights until my arms became noodles, stretching my chest three times a day, and ultimately becoming who I was before the surgery. Being an active child and High School Athlete, I felt a desire to participate with my team. Despite the surgery eliminating my basketball season, fortunately the volleyball season fell in the spring. Many of my friends and even coaches doubted that I would even try out for the upcoming season. These accusations only fueled my fire to work harder and rise to my potential. My junior year I enlisted as the starting middle blocker and was awarded first team all-league by the various league coaches. At the time I knew the reason why I performed with a vast amount of determination was a result of people not placing belief in me. However, reminiscing on these events, I realized the hours of work and countless times of picking myself up, were not for the nonbelievers, but for me. The reminder I receive from peering into a mirror gazing at the six inch scar coating my chest, presents a tiny smirk to my face, and a warm feeling in my heart.

Danny Meritt is a mechanical engineering major.

CONSIDER THIS

- *Like Meritt, you may have started essays with dictionary definitions. Does the first sentence of this essay engage the audience in a meaningful and/or effective manner? Does it add anything to the essay? What would happen if the essay actually started with the second sentence—or even the second paragraph?*
- *The author tries to communicate his pain, suffering, and perseverance to the audience. Does he do more "showing" or "telling"? At times the narrative seems a bit convoluted—could this be seen as a direct stylistic choice by Meritt to involve the audience in his post-surgery state of mind and emotions? How might you use the same technique in your own essay?*

Backpacking Through Life

Trevor Elsbree

We went 11 days without a shower; 11 days in the same clothes; 11 days without civilization. We crossed glaringly bright glaciers at 9,000 feet, swam in crystal clear, snow-melt lakes, forded raging creeks and waded in tranquil streams. My friends and I trekked for 120 miles through the granite peaks and alpine lakes of the Trinity Alps Wilderness. The trip, which equally overwhelmed and exhausted us, left my friends and I feeling victorious and accomplished.

I love coming back from each backpacking trip with spectacular memories despite the blood, sweat and corporeal punishment. The overwhelming sense of accomplishment far outweighs any temporary memories of physical discomfort which would prevent me from returning. I can think of many times on that historic 11 day trip when I wanted to be home surrounded by comfort instead of in the rugged circumstances I had found myself in. Over the course of that 120 mile trip, our party encountered many roadblocks. I wouldn't trade the unforgettable and uncomfortable memories of that trip for anything. One miserable night we found ourselves huddled on a granite shelf in a lightning storm. We could practically kiss the lightening around us. Looking back on that situation, I remember the courage we all had to find, the sense of bravery we needed to endure. That experience made me feel as if I lived through a priceless moment.

Whenever I think of the Trinity Alps Wilderness, the first things that jump to mind are adventure, conquest and a rebirth of my affinity with nature. The Trinity Alps Wilderness—a region of Northern California largely untouched by the pursuits of man—is a destination spot known for world class backpacking and mountaineering. The Alps, perfect for the intrepid outdoors-man and thrill seeking traveler, were practically my backyard growing up. I hold the Trinity Alps' danger and excitement in my heart.

LOOK HERE

"Visit" the Trinity Alps through the adventures of blogger James Mitchell who blogs about his expeditions: http://trinityalpsphoto.blogspot.com

Ever since I was old enough to carry a backpack, my parents have been dragging me along on wilderness treks. Like it or not, over time my parents taught me an appreciation and love for the outdoors. Growing up, I did not have experience to know what I could learn to love. Like all kids, I was unable to make important decisions for myself because I lacked wisdom and understanding. I didn't know or care why schooling was important, or why my parents pushed me so much to play sports and participate in activities I didn't enjoy. They "strongly encouraged" me to play baseball and soccer, to go "play outside," and to take guitar lessons. I vividly remember being dragged along on countless hiking trips when vacationing at various national parks. While I can't say that everything they convinced me to experience was a success, (I still hate baseball and never have had the patience to play music), I can say that I have played soccer for more than ten years and have nurtured an amazing love for the outdoors and backpacking. Looking back on growing up I can thank my parents for the efforts they made to help me discover what it was that I loved doing.

I am thankful that my mom and dad made sure I "sampled the buffet" of experiences life had to offer. I can't help but wonder how different a person I might have become without my passion for the outdoors. Backpackers and avid outdoor adventurers alike share a belief that nature provides an experience that can't be found elsewhere. There exists a universal bond shared by those you pass by on a backpacking trail. People who backpack are hardy and must be willing to eschew many basic comforts in exchange for an escape from mundane urban society—a quality often unique to backpackers because not many people are willing to brave such extremes for enjoyment. Passing by a complete stranger deep in the wilderness I can smile and know simply based on the both of us meeting we have so much more in common than the average passerby on the street.

My last years of backpacking demonstrate my growth as an individual. My friends and I have gone from being mere passengers on our backpacking trips to taking on the roles of pilot, navigator, and captain all in one. The summer before my junior year of high school my friends and I decided to go on a trip without any adults. I can imagine the decision to allow five 16 year-olds to venture into the wilderness alone must have been difficult for our parents, but it was a milestone journey both physically and mentally.

Part of what makes backpacking so special lies in the concept of carrying everything you need to survive for days on end. The need to wear everything and anything you might need is equally nerve wracking and empowering. Any wilderness foray requires careful planning and thoughtful execution because at the end of the day you are alone in nature. Never had this point been so clear until the trip was my own to plan. You truly understand and appreciate the logistics that go into every detail, such as where and what you will eat for every meal. This attention to detail starkly contrasts from the ignorant bliss of childhood. No longer can you be an oblivious observer when faced with the reality of being responsible for your own survival as the most critical display of adulthood.

I find it impossible to watch myself grow. It's easy to look back and say I became an adult on my 18th birthday. Thankfully however, growing up isn't arbitrarily served to you. The process of maturing into an adult happens so gradually, (and at least for me will happen over the course of far more than 18 years). I find that only at certain spontaneous moments are you given perspective into your true age. In these moments I feel as if I am shoved into the body of a stranger and shown my life through an outside window.

Looking at backpacking presents the most obvious evidence of growth for me personally. By comparing the subtle changes of each year's trip my progression becomes apparent. I started these trips as a child and ended with the most recent one right before I moved away for college. I went from being dependent upon my parents for planning and execution to being a fully equal partner with my dad on my most recent Trinity Alps adventure.

Ever since that 11 day trip with my friends I wanted to revisit some of the lakes and incredible peaks we climbed. This past Labor Day my dad and I planned one last trip in the Trinity Alps before I went off to college. My dad made this last trip unique because we planned it together. This transformation felt like the last growth beyond my childhood years into an older state of adulthood because he treated me as an equal out of respect for my abilities and maturity.

For this last trip my dad and I decided to visit my favorite lake in all the Trinity Alps. Grizzly Lake, which I first visited on my 120 mile trip years ago, is the hardest lake in the entire wilderness to get to. Not only does Grizzly Lake sit at higher elevation than any other lake but its waters also lie beneath the tallest point in the Trinity Alps mountain range, Thompson Peak. To top it all off, the journey up Grizzly Creek to the lake places you in a picturesque mountain valley with the occasional tantalizing glimpse of the waterfall and mountaineering ahead. When I was much younger I remember feelings of intimidation looking at the rocky and very steep climb up to Grizzly Lake. This past trip my dad and I took the ascent to a whole new level. We scaled past the lake and above to the summit of Thompson Peak.

Ditching our heavy packs and wielding our ice axes we climbed past the glacier and steep snow fields above Grizzly. The ascent was slow and treacherous. One small slip and you were sliding down the steep snow towards the abrupt rocky ending of the slippery slope. After we finally crossed the north facing snow and crevasse fields my dad and I found ourselves staring up at the base of the rock face that rose to the peak. The climb took us two hours. We hauled our way past treacherous rock slides, and up conveniently placed trees until we reached the spine of the ridge that sloped up precariously to the peak.

We eventually made it to the peak, climbed the last spire, and ate lunch gazing for miles in every direction. I took my pictures and couldn't help but think about how much had changed since the last time I had seen Grizzly Lake below me. The lake was incredible and still by far my favorite, but still nothing like I remembered it. I felt changed yet still awed by the natural beauty I looked down on. I felt the strength of the mountains and the incredible sense of all that they had given me over the years. I knew that I would be facing new adventures in life but that the lessons in self-reliance would always be part of who I am.

Trevor Elsbree is a computer engineering major.

CONSIDER THIS

- *Elsbree begins his essay describing his 120 mile backpacking trip with friends, and ends by discussing a similar trip with his father. How do these two stories work together to develop the writer's overall focus on "change"? Do his stories enhance each other—and the essay? Does he effectively transition between each experience?*
- *How do Elsbree's descriptions of the Trinity Alps complement the changes that he sees in himself? Are there any specific details of the landscape—descriptive or stylistic moments—that particularly speak to Elsbree's experiences?*

Artificial Experience

Munir Eltal

"What kind of doctor do you wanna be when you grow up?" I don't know. "Why did you pick Biomedical Engineering?" I don't know. "Isn't Biomedical Engineering hard?" I don't care. My peers bombard me with these types of questions daily and my answers do little to satisfy them. There's nothing in my past to suggest that I was destined to be a Biomedical Engineer or doctor. My dad is a Civil Engineer and deals with nonliving materials for his job, while my mom works at a daycare center and nurses infants. Heck, there isn't a single member of my extended family that works as anything close to a doctor. There have been moments in my life where I have been faced with different types of medical care, but my experiences are distressing enough that they should have deterred me from the path I've chosen. Everyone has *that one* story to tell about how they *knew* that their major was right for them; mine is a lot more traumatic than it is inspiring.

"Woooh! Woooh!" It is a particularly overcast day in the middle of August and the high-pitched horn of the train can be heard in the distance. Michael is about two steps ahead of me, trying his best to stay balanced along the metal rails of the train tracks. His long blond hair covers his ears and the wind is doing just enough so that I can catch glimpses of his covered eyes. Summer vacation is fast coming to an end, and we want to do something special to remember our final month before we go to high school. "Wooooh! Wooooh!" The train is a bit louder now, but it is still not close enough to have to worry about it. Michael stops and turns to me, gives me a smirk, and marches forward again at a slightly faster pace. He always gets this way when he is about to do something crazy. I want to say I don't care, but today I am doing that "something crazy" with him. I am not one for taking too many risks; however Michael has me convinced that I will make a lot more friends in high school if I have an "awesome" story to tell everyone. My teenage mind can't argue with that logic. Again the train blows its horn, but this time I can see it start to materialize over the horizon. We arrive out our destination with time to spare. We stand on a bridge about fifteen feet high with the Merced River directly below us. The water is warm this time of year, but more importantly, it is deep enough for us to jump into. "WOOOH! WOOOH!" The train is about two minutes away now. I look over at Michael who still has that same smirk on his face. Neither of us has said a thing since getting on the tracks, but we both know what the other is thinking. The first one to jump will forever give up his right to tell the story. I usually would not mind, but I know that with Michael, each retelling of the story will be more and more exaggerated. At first I will have jumped just ten seconds before the train got to us. Then it will become a whole minute. Then two minutes. Next, the train will not even have been in view yet. And the story will be retold again and again until I am not in the story altogether. I can't let that happen. Our feet are shaking now with the force of the freight train coming towards us. Five seconds until impact: I'm starting to sweat and Michael hasn't even blinked an eye. Four seconds until impact: My heart is bursting from the adrenaline pumping through me, and still not a single movement from Michael. Three seconds until impact: I don't care who tells the story and I fall to the safety of the river. To this day I still don't know if I really heard it, but even under the water I swear I could just catch the muffled screams of Michael as he leapt from the railing a half second too late.

It's October 30th and, as with my entire high school career, I've procrastinated on this college application for far too long. It doesn't help that I have friends with the same poor work ethic as me either. To my right sits Michael, one hand typing away, the other plastic and immobile in his lap. My application to Cal Poly San Luis Obispo is complete but for one question. Which major would I like to declare? Or more accurately, how would I like to spend the rest of my life? I don't know. How could anyone know as a sixteen-year-old? I look over to Michael to see what he's chosen. Nothing. Out of the corner of my eye I catch Michael scratching his prosthetic finger. Even after all these years I still find it quite disturbing. He says it's his "phantom hand" that he is scratching. His nervous system still thinks that he has a limb there and occasionally tells his body that he needs to itch it. I scroll down the page of majors offered at Cal Poly until I find my cursor hovering over "Biomedical Engineering." The name sounds pretty cool, but what do they do? One Google search later, I am a self-made expert on the subject. It turns out that Biomedical Engineers work with artificial organs, medical devices, and *prosthetic limbs*. I take another quick glance at Michael's hand and recall all the times he's complained about it. It's too rigid. It doesn't hold anything. The artificial skin color doesn't match his real skin. How hard can these problems be to solve? I guess I know one sure-fire way to find out.

They're hard. And by hard, I mean that even after two years of a college education I am still no closer to solving these problems than I was before coming here. I have some ideas, but I don't have the knowledge necessary to implement them. In the meantime, Michael has been at UCLA and is already doing research as a Microbiologist. You would think that he would have chosen to be a Biomedical Engineer too, but he said he couldn't "do all the math and physics engineers gotta do. It's too hard!" It's not *that* hard, but I'll never let him know that, just as I'll never let him know that his actions are what push me to succeed. His negligence is what motivates me. I'm not sure why, but I feel this need to make up for his lack of effort. It's his fault he got hit by the train, but I feel this obligation to act on it. He doesn't know this though, and every time he tells the story of the train it gets more and more dramatic. I make up for it by updating him on my schooling. Every time I tell him about my classes they seem to be getting exponentially harder. From pop quizzes, to pop midterms, and finally to pop finals. Until one day I'll retell the story and I'll be the one teaching the class. And all this wouldn't have happened if I didn't jump first.

Munir Eltal is a Biomedical Engineering major.

CONSIDER THIS

- *Eltal's second paragraph is quite long—longer than most paragraphs need to be. However, a longer paragraph can occasionally work in an essay, especially if the writer wants to achieve a specific effect. What is the effect of Eltal's second paragraph? How does the length of this paragraph help develop the content?*
- *All incoming Cal Poly students select a major upon entry. What major did you choose? Who or what influenced you when making this decision?*

Profiles

Who or what has been influential in your life?

[I took] this image of Morgan Geiger. . . . To my surprise she hadn't known that I took this, so the emotions in this image are real to me. Again, the idea of solitude and wanting that "alone time" can be seen here.

Taken during a photo-shoot for one of my friends with a passion for music, I was setting up and I noticed [Megan] singing quietly so I snapped this photograph without her knowing. Because the photo was taken candidly, I was able to grab straight emotion from her. The look on her face shows contentment and relaxation, as she is doing what she loves, in the environment she loves. The idea of being alone, as you can see, isn't always negative.

Visually speaking . . . the image [is] shown in black and white, not to save on color ink, but to act as a messenger. . . .Usually, when looking at photographs, a black and white image has much more visual impact emotionally because of how simple the image is; there are no colors to distract the viewer from the true emotions of the subject in the photo.

David Jang took this photo and wrote this brief analysis. David is a forestry and natural resources major.

WRITER'S MEMO

I was very surprised to be granted time for an interview within President Armstrong's schedule. I dressed nice, brought a voice recorder and some notes, and left my Stats class early to bike over to the Admin building for my appointment. At this point, my writing assignment was already a success—I had the opportunity to meet with my university's President! The essay flowed well and I finished it early, although I quickly became tired of listening to my voice while I reviewed our recorded talk. This interview essay turned out to be a very rewarding assignment.

The Right Guy for Right Now

Caleb Knight

On the fourth floor of Cal Poly's Administration building, overlooking the effects of strong decisions and implemented policies, sits a man who shies away from personal glory or praise. He greets his secretary and office visitors with broad smiles and shows visible excitement to begin his daily executive work. Such behavior provokes a question: is optimism a help or a hindrance? It's associated with happiness, which America pursues. It lowers stress levels, which, left unchecked, can cause negative strains on mental and physical health. It's strongly supported by a singing electric fish in many restaurants and stores, who writhes in place while urging me not to worry. Despite these facts, many leaders preach against optimism, claiming it blinds people to impending hardship and causes an "ignorance is bliss" mentality. President Jeffrey Armstrong of Cal Poly reiterates this thought, saying "blind optimism can lead to crushing failure" near the end of his Fall Conference speech to his staff. Directly after, however, President Armstrong claims to be an optimist himself, yet says he is "realistic about what our challenges are." A realistically optimistic view when considering future challenges is more professionally effective than blind optimism. To close his speech, Armstrong invites his faculty and staff to make the same choice he has made—to choose to believe in Cal Poly's future and to work together to realize his vision of the university shining across the world as a beacon of excellence. President Jeffrey Armstrong affects many people around him by leading his staff and students with this vision and by modeling the grounded, humble character of a realistic optimist with an established set of values.

Mr. Armstrong is almost as new to Cal Poly as I am, yet the reasons he was selected during one of the worst periods of financial duress the university has ever faced quickly became evident while I spoke with him. Dressed in a dark jacket, slacks, reading glasses, and a smile, the new president invited me into his office for an interview as a friend and an equal—offering a handshake, a pat on the back, and a plush seat. He certainly seemed to belong among the dark-stained walnut shelves, thick surfaced desk, and old books that filled his large office. The big leather chair by his desk was positioned askew—obviously recently occupied—but he left the chair and a few scattered papers at the desk to fill a seat close to mine. We made simple, basic conversation about my major and move-in, but soon enough I had to know—what makes him different? What made the university hire him? Without failing to mention how honored he is to even have the job or how the university was built to where it is today by many other astounding leaders, Mr. Armstrong summed up his thoughts, saying, "the main thing is, I'm the right guy for now."

Though other presidents were perfect for other times, Armstrong had the experience and outlook necessary and appropriate for leading this world-changing university through now. As I'd later conclude, some of his answers seemed at first to be too concise and too easy to be true. After him saying how he is the right guy for now, I was thinking, "But 'now' is a very difficult time!" However, he went on to qualify himself by his past experiences with tough budgets and higher education challenges, all the while "remaining optimistic and looking to the future." Mr. Armstrong would break eye contact with me to gaze at what might have been a reflective auto-biography in his mind's eye, but he would return from his pensive trance with a smile, a nod, and a complete answer. "Good news is, I'm from Michigan," he said, chuckling while thinking about his years spent in higher education there, "Bad news is, I'm from Michigan." He used this contradicting explanation to reflect how, though challenges like Michigan's constant budget crises are bad, they also prepared him and taught him how to respond to difficulties he would face in his future—a preparation that had a large role in winning him this prestigious job.

LOOK HERE

Given the current budget crisis in education, university presidents are facing unprecedented challenges. Check out Jeremi Suri's recent CNN.com article about the difficulties facing university presidents: http://www.cnn.com/2012/06/19/opinion/suri-public-universities/index.html

Though in his optimism he looks toward the future, he says he is more concerned with the short term, hence illustrating an important lesson in a selective near-sightedness essential for working through challenges. Even when considering short-term challenges, he says he is still optimistic because he works with "really good people in this building, as well as the deans, department chairs, [and] faculty . . . working . . . to bring you a great education." As the head of the university, he never forgets to acknowledge the many other essential parts that compose his school's body. To conclude his answer on how he responds to Cal Poly's difficulties, Mr. Armstrong reminded me to "always rise above your circumstances and affect what you can affect. Some things you can't change . . . Do your best to work around it, or change the other things that you can change to move forward." This is a key factor of the president's optimistic approach to issues—his realism. He works hard to change and affect what he can, but if the cause is lost, he wastes no time complaining about it. Instead, he finds ways to work around the issues to continue pushing towards his goals for the university. Examples of this are the ever-present school-wide problems of partying and sexual assaults. Knowing that it isn't in his power to remove these problems from his campus, he attacks them indirectly through many awareness and safety presentations for incoming students, so they may know how to respond in potentially dangerous situations. Treating these problems as immortal enemies, Armstrong doesn't waste time trying to kill them. Instead, he arms his listeners with weapons of knowledge so that the enemies will show their ugly heads less often, and the university may continue to progress forward towards goals of education and graduation.

Mr. Armstrong was obviously full of advice and strategic knowledge from decades of professional experience in higher education, but to fully understand the motives behind the actions, I pried into his mind, searching for the character behind the professional personality: his values as a man. A leader's core values should be very important to his followers, as they reflect the basis of decisions and policy trends and provide a blueprint for replication and change in one's own life. When asked how the increased responsibilities and pressures of the presidency have changed him, Mr. Armstrong negated the very assumption of the question. Rather than changing him, he said, "[the position] reinforced some of the best parts of me . . . it's made me appreciate my family more." After a significant move from Michigan and leaving his grown kids, he has found himself missing them and finding greater enjoyment in their visits. Noticing how family was referred to as the "best parts of him," I had to follow the answer with a more general question concerning the top three principles he uses to prioritize his busy and important life. After thought, family fell to second: "I grew up in the Bible Belt . . . so I have a certain set of beliefs that are . . . very important to me: so Faith [would be most important]. Then second would be family." The distinction seemed clear and established, and as third, Mr. Armstrong chose his constant effort "to make a difference, and treat others the way I'd like to be treated." However, quickly after the three, he assured me that all are "intertwined . . . they're all really similar. It's my value set."

Mr. Armstrong reinforced his proclaimed value set through other answers and also by his body language throughout the interview. From the initial courteous handshake to the smiles and attentive head-turns and nods throughout our talk, his natural sense of hospitality was apparent. By the time I asked for his top three life-arranging principles, he had already referenced the "Golden Rule" twice yet reiterated it a third time, so I would understand his emphasis on it. His faith was better hidden, which is understandable as a man of importance—he wouldn't want to be tied to a certain denomination or religious stereotype that would cause his critics to make judgments about him before hearing him out. However, Jesus claimed the second greatest commandment of Moses was to love one's neighbor as himself (trumped only by loving God with everything), so the president's policy of treating others how he would want to be treated fit perfectly in line with the teachings of the Word. Finally, Mr. Armstrong said, "the best thing I ever did was . . . ask my wife to marry me, 'cause there's all sorts of other things that stem from that: my daughter getting married, both kids being born . . . That was a pretty awesome step . . . in the right direction." This conclusion again highlighted his belief that his family was the best part of him. I truly did not need to ask for his three defining principles—Mr. Armstrong strongly reflected his love for his family, his commitment to making a difference and honoring the Golden Rule, and his Biblical beliefs through his other answers and character-reflective mannerisms. Feeling like I now had a comprehensive sense of my President's character, I began to self-reflect and wonder if I had defined answers for my own difficult questions. It became clear that life values and priorities are important for the pursuit of any position, and Armstrong had spoken with such a confidence in his that I could easily see how a hiring board or a crowd of students would be affected and inspired by his character.

With a firmly grounded value set as well as the necessary experience, Mr. Armstrong will lead Cal Poly to graduate thousands of students yearly who carry the potential to change the world in many ways. This influence of the university's president is exponentially increased with his graduates taking up positions of their own throughout the world. When asked if he has begun to see effects of his influence yet, Mr. Armstrong looked away and nodded slowly, saying, "Yes, yes I have. I've received a lot of positive comments;" with this, he moved forward in his seat and leaned towards me, continuing, "and I think a lot of people feel like we're heading in the right direction . . . I'm very pleased with where we are." Again, humility shone through his soft-spoken, vaguely descriptive answer, as he was careful to quickly switch his subject from "I" to "We." This subject change reinforces his emphasis on the school body as a whole and the importance of working with his faculty and students together toward common goals. He constantly shifts the attention from himself to others, whether they are his faculty and staff, his family, his wife, or the entire Cal Poly school body. This dichotomy of power in humility is a recipe for effective leadership also demonstrated by Jesus of the Bible Armstrong was taught from. People turn open ears to intelligent men who are not eager to earn personal acclaim and admiration.

President Jeffrey Armstrong speaks with strong words yet affects many people also by his reflection of character and positive thinking. The best parents are not those who raise children who trust and rely on them completely, but rather children who are independent and instilled with character traits that prepare them for the outside world. In the same way, President Armstrong knows Cal Poly's goals should revolve around "success for all students . . . and figuring out how [they're] going to be the best . . . in this environment." Even after less than an hour with this man, I developed a mold through which my own success is attainable. This mold consists of a firmly established set of values, a constantly positive outlook towards the short term and long term, proper knowledge and experience for a desired field, and humility enough to not only constantly shift attention to my supporters, but to thrice mention to a student interviewer how honored he is to be the subject of a freshman's essay.

Caleb Knight is a Kinesiology major.

WORK CITED

Armstrong, Jeffrey. Personal Interview. 3 October 2011.

CONSIDER THIS

- *Knight approached his interview with a very specific goal in mind: to better understand President Armstrong's values and priorities. Do you think he successfully explored this focus in his profile? Did his profile have a clear "angle"?*
- *President Armstrong is clearly an influential figure in Cal Poly students' lives—often in ways students don't fully understand. If you had an opportunity to interview President Armstrong, what would you want to know? Did Knight provide you with the "insider's perspective" that helped you better understand President Armstrong's role on campus?*

Follow-up Interview with President Armstrong

What role does writing play in the work of a college president?
It's huge. On a regular basis I'm drafting and composing e-mails. So it's huge. On a more formal basis, [there's] communication with various groups, as well as the campus community, communication with donors, letters to individuals who have had horrible things happen—there's a constant flow of communication. Constant flow of letters that leave the office.

How much time do you spend writing each day?
If you count what I spend on e-mail, I spend several hours a day. Mary Fiala [Assistant to the Chief of Staff] keeps up with people, awards, all different types of things, and so she'll write letters for me. And then [the] Development [office] writes letters. My Chief of Staff, Betsy [Kinsley], and I will write letters. I'll compose or I'll draft notes sometimes and just send them. Sometimes I'll send them, [or someone will] then edit, put it in better format, but if something is of particular importance, the Provost may review it, the Chief of Staff may review it, or the Chief of Staff may draft it and say, "this is what I think you should do." So it flows all different ways.

That leads me to another question: what is your writing process like? It sounds like you write multiple drafts.
It's all over the place. Sometimes it's very simple—compose and hit send. To the very far end, if we're working on something, you know, a report that will go out on fall conference [week], we'll start on that weeks in advance. And so it's sort of writing by committee.

Learning to write collaboratively is important. But to be a member of the team, you have to have your own strengths. So [some] say, "you're in the position as president, a lot of people do your writing for you." Well, that's true, but I had to do a lot of writing over the years to get to this position.

Would you say that you enjoy writing?
Yeah, I do. I like composing and laying out thoughts. Strategy. What we may be doing with a particular set of donors—I may be writing a note. I also like, you know, writing a first draft of a speech and thinking about what I'm going to say. Having said that, I don't write speeches a lot; normally, I'll just simply think about what I'm going to say and I'll put it in bullet form. For more formal speeches, I have Chip Visci [Director of Communications], who works in our office, he will write a lot. We got to know each other very, very quickly, so he picked up on my

style—my speaking style. I try to have my writing reflect my speaking style because I don't like to be two different people.

Would you describe your style as casual?
Yeah. It is. Most of the regular correspondence via emails is more casual. And then there's all sorts of formal communications, form letters. And then, of course, for graduation, that script's been written and revised every year. But, this year, we spent—a good example—is the charge to the graduates. I wrote pieces of that last year, he edited this year. He edited and I rewrote parts of it, so it was collaborative writing. And we ended up with a five minute charge to the graduates.

I know you're a very busy person, but do you ever have time to write for pleasure?
From time to time, I have kept a journal. I don't do it very much now, just due to time. But I write e-mails to my daughter and my son. And I will write some [ideas] related to work, some thoughts and what I think I'm going to do—but it's only for me.

There have been different periods of time where I kept a journal, especially when I was into something new and challenging and at the end of the day or the beginning of the day, I would write. When my kids were young, I kept a journal. In fact, it was a journal I bought at Disneyland and I still have it. I talked about each of the kids at different ages, just intimate thoughts. One of these days I will give it to them to read.

So here's my final question: do you have any advice or thoughts that you can offer first-year students who are learning to write in college?
Writing is very important. The digital world does not replace the need to form your thoughts, do it properly, get it on paper—however you do that. No matter what you do, you've got to be a skilled communicator, and that means the written word as well as verbal.

Any other thoughts?
I don't think so . . . . [pause] A lot my writing has been scientific. The other thing that I've been involved with, and there's examples of it—I was involved for many years as a physiologist, so I wrote a lot of scientific papers. But then in the last 10 or 12 years, I was involved with social responsibility in the food chain, so I published quite a few opinion pieces, and, really, pieces where I was trying to influence and get people to change. So I could share some of those with you . . . . [For instance,] several years ago, [I wrote] a message to some egg producers: don't confuse change to caving to animal rights activists. But you should change—you need to change.

That would be great. I can share them with instructors and they can share them with students.
Oh yeah, yeah! They can critique them! Plenty to critique!

Interview conducted June 28, 2012 by Brenda Helmbrecht.

CONSIDER THIS

After the interview, the interviewer was left with an audio recording of the interview (she used her IPhone to record the discussion). She then had to take the audio file and transform it into a written text. She added appropriate punctuation, paragraph breaks, and, using brackets, she added a few words to help readers follow the discussion. The goal is to recreate the conversation as accurately as possible; none of the president's language was changed. After your interview, you, too, will need to reconstruct a verbal conversation using writing. You may find that your skills as a writer are challenged in new ways.

WRITER'S MEMO

Writing this essay brought me great joy and happiness. I didn't make any outlines and only read over the instructions once or twice. I remember staring at my computer in my dorm and focusing all of my thoughts on the moment when I had planted my first tree. From there, my hands did the rest. I enjoy and relate to description and to the use of pathos in essays, so I wanted to be sure to include as much of these two components as I could throughout my own essay. My goal was to share my thoughts and ideas of change through explaining how my own thoughts were created. I recommend you to not skim over this essay. If you start with a calm and peaceful mindset, I believe that you will get the reaction that I experienced while writing it. I hope by the end of reading my essay you are left with a more positive outlook towards everyday life and the idea of change itself.

A Seed of Change

Keri Forsberg

Have you ever realized that studying outside helps you concentrate and remember things? That the cool breeze combing through the leaves of the branches as they dance back and forth, making a '*shhhhhh*' sound, helps you stay calm and concentrated? Then, as you move your senses away from the trees, you find yourself concentrating on the sunbeams forcing you to close your eyes as the warmth wraps around your body. You open your eyes taking a deep breath as the warmth deepens past your skin, warming your soul, making you feel a part of something much greater than yourself. Positivity emerges and you ask yourself, "Why don't I come out here more often?"

Centralized in a world of concrete walls, asphalt playgrounds, and high-rise buildings, we are forced to underestimate the power of nature and how much of an impact it can have on our ability to learn. Learning as a child from the world around us that there is *a place* for trees, *a place* for parks, *a place* to read a book, *a place* to go and listen to the trees—*a place* that we usually have to drive to that is not our home or school.

LOOK HERE

See how volunteers are supporting growth in San Luis Obispo County: http://onecoolearth.net/category/take-action

But what if we could change that? What if we could help bring together both worlds of school and park? A seed: that is all you need—a tree seed that would add some lively green to the overwhelming grey asphalt. I am proud to say that I saw this exact change occur in Long Beach, California, at Lowell Elementary School. I am more proud to say that my father, Eric Forsberg, a common citizen, was the leader of and reason that this project was started and completed. He fought for what he believed in, which was to make the school a better place for his children. In doing so he made blueprints, found assistance from other students' parents, and didn't take no for an answer. When I asked him why this project took so long to be approved of by the school, he responded with a chuckle saying, "Small minded people get in the way of something that's good . . . I don't take the word 'no,' It's just not in my vocabulary."

After months of planning, organizing, and raising enough money, my father was finally able to plant over four hundred trees. He not only was successful in planting trees at Lowell Elementary, but also at the adjoining middle school. "Hundreds of volunteers showed up," my dad proudly stated, "kids of all ages, parents, grandparents, teachers and students" all came out to plant a tree " . . . . it was a big deal!"

I was one of those kids and I will never forget that day. Feeling so proud that I was the daughter of the man who made such a large, significant change to my school—a change that will grow on forever. I remember my dad whispering in my ear after I had finished planting my tree and saying, "Now you can say that you have made a contribution to this school. As you grow, it will grow, and you will never forget it. Now, you will pass by this school and someday you will realize the impact of what we have done today and how easy it is to make a difference in the community, as long as you put your mind to it."

Change is not easy. It takes work and time—time that most people do not want to deal with. Although they might have the drive in the beginning to start a project, it takes will and determination to accomplish it. I connect change to helping others and making a difference. The impact that was made in the community that day will forever be engraved in my mind, and I will always be reminded of it as I drive past my ever-growing tree. The trees now line the perimeter of the joint schools, tall enough to provide vast amounts of shade and comfort to those passing by. The internally dispersed trees help to make the blacktop more inviting to those who wish to only read or sit outside during recess or lunch. The view outside the second story windows are now full of trees, which act as shades to the ever warming classrooms, making it easier to bring nature up close.

"Make Things Better" said a sign on a random building that I found. For some odd reason those words struck me when I read them. "Make things better." That's all it said, and that's all it needed to say. Sometimes that's all one needs to hear and be reminded of once and a while. We as humans are constantly trying to make things better all of the time—be it with a relationship, our body image, personality, friendships, grades, community, or our impact on the world. With small acts of 'making things better,' we can all help to change the world. The more little things that we accomplish, the larger the impact we will see. Even an act of something as small as planting a tree can grow and be cherished for generations.

When I am outside, as I often am, I find myself taking in everything more than I used to. Listening, watching, and observing the small things that people don't normally pay attention to. The small details and shadows that are based on the large, more noticeable features of a landscape are what give it depth and life; it would not be complete without them. Just like the world wouldn't be the same without people like my father, or a small sign with a large message. We are all capable of making a difference and all have equally important roles in making this world a better place. How might you start this movement you ask?

I might start with a seed, that's what seemed to change me.

Keri Forsberg is a recreation, parks, and tourism major.

- *Forsberg threads her impressions of trees throughout her essay. Find at least three different manifestations of tree imagery used at different points in the essay. How do these images enhance her notion of change?*
- *Think of a community effort in which you have been involved as volunteer, as a recipient, or even as an observant bystander. Take five minutes to brainstorm and jot down key episodes, or moments, which could describe the experience to an outside observer. From this brainstorm session, can you find a dominant impression or angle which you could use to launch into drafting an essay?*

WRITER'S MEMO

This essay was a thrill for me to write. I wanted to incorporate some sort of connection between superheroes and my friend's passion about writing. At first I wanted to write the essay like a story and incorporate the quotes I wanted to use from the interview as her personal thoughts and dreams, but I changed it into more of a timeline-story that starts from the beginning of her writing career. This gave me more of a chance to write about her journey of writing with a glimpse of her personality, as opposed to just a timeline of who she is and what she does.

Look in the sky! It's a bird! It's a plane! It's … Liz Nuno?

Brianne St. Pierre

Once upon a time there was a young girl. She inhaled books like pieces of decadent chocolate. Her passion to read enhanced her vocabulary and allowed her imagination to split open and spill over paper. One day, she ran out of things to read. *Oh no! What should I do?* she asked herself. Since she read all the books available to her, she couldn't fulfill her thirst. Thirsty every day, something needed to change. But what? Pondering, she grabbed for a piece of paper and a pen. *If I cannot read, I shall write my own stories*, she announced to herself. Ever since then, she has been writing fantasy, semi-romantic action packed stories. This girl now is in college, and currently traveling abroad in England to explore the world of English. Her name is Liz Nuno. Super Woman of writing stories.

This Super Woman of Writing is one of my best friends. I have known Liz for practically my whole life, since she is my sister's best friend also. Growing up with her meant sharing the experience of writing collaborative stories with her. The creativity and ideas that she effortlessly plops out of her head never cease to disappoint. Of course, like everyone, she had a journey to get where she is today. Like a classic superhero story. Let's rewind this story to a younger time.

It is middle school. The brilliant sun shrinks beneath the horizon, and the stars commence their dazzling. Liz sits at her desk. Thinking. She needs to occupy her mind with something. After reading all the books in her own personal library, she needs to fulfill her thirst for words. A grand thought jolts into her head. "Alas! I shall write 'a fantasy book with a bit of romance thrown in, [because] we live in the real world; why read and write about it?'" she exclaimed to the world. It was in this moment that Liz Nuno transformed into Super Woman. Ever since then, she created a goal: to combat vile, dreary life with powerful words of quest, a little dash of sweetheart romance, and extreme description, with anticipation that one day her "[desire] to be the source of someone's inspiration" will be satisfied.

Feeding off inspiration from novels, she gains insight to an idea, sits, and begins her writing process. Jotting vigorously, Liz writes. Simply writes. Yes, she "[has] a basic idea of what [she wants] to happen," but "in the end, it's how the story comes … sometimes [she wants] it to go one way, but it goes another way." This is the beauty of writing. Even though a mere idea or image may not be depicted as one would wish, it can transform into a whole new meaning, scene, or deceptive plot. Taking a thought or a momentary idea and transforming it into copious amounts of stunning language and intellect is astounding.

Not only does the transformation of thoughts and ideas come together to create a story, but the characters do as well. Her ideology behind characters is to put herself in the situation, pretending to feel, smell, hear, and notice what is going on around her. This allows her to write on a more personal level. An excellent example from her short story titled *Joy* is, "After they would run and prance and roll in the meadows, her mother would take her to the stream and they would stick their feet in where the current was strongest, feeling the fish tickle their toes." Description such as this is not obtained by thoughtlessness and words randomly tossed on a piece of paper, but of pure contemplation while closing your eyes and teleporting yourself into the shoes of the character. This creates a very intimate bond between the reader and the writer. It is rather intriguing that her style of writing includes transforming into a new person just to tickle a reader's need for entertainment. Although this may appear effortless, beware of the demons!

Of course, writing can be cumbersome, and at times quite troublesome. Fighting off the writing demons (also known as writer's block), Liz "[does] not like that sometimes it takes a while for inspiration to come." Being patient is the key to the door of writing. The fact is, one day writing just flows out of the mind, like blood oozes out of a cut. On other days, the thoughts stay inside, like a stubborn child who protests to enjoying the pleasant, lovely day and plays video games instead. At times, this writing demon overshadows Liz's concentration to a point where "[she wants] to write, but [she has] no words." Breaking out in a cold sweat, trying to save each thought onto a piece of paper before the villain arrives, hope is lost. Or so it seems. Other ways to shield from the attack of the beast is to rewrite current stories or even ancient ones. Liz "usually . . . [writes sentences] out on paper and then [fixes them]...usually [by] rephrasing . . . but sometimes [she'll] rewrite the whole scene." This technique allows her the opportunity to reread her work, improve it, and gain more insight on how she wishes the story to be. The monster has been conquered.

Let's press the fast forward button. After years of discovering a favorable art form, conquering writing demons, and establishing a suitable writing method, Liz wishes either to become an author, or an editor of novels. Even though she does not know 100 percent what she would like to do with all her words and ideas, all she wants is to be involved with books. Out of all careers, why choose an author or editor? Isn't sitting and writing just tedious? Liz strays from the pack of the 'I hate writing' wolves, and releases from her heart that she "loves reading about people's adventures" which instills a majestic hunger in her soul to "want to have some of [her] own [adventures]" through writing.

LOOK HERE

Give in to your writing spirit and submit your creative literary pursuits to Cal Poly's annual creative writing contest. All majors are invited to participate. Winners are awarded cash prizes and are published in the Byzantium *magazine:*
http://cla.calpoly.edu/engl_contest.html

Not only does she want to produce her own adventures, she wants to persevere like her favorite author Jane Austen. Another author that inspires her is JK Rowling. Connection? They were both rejected at first, but obviously these two authors made it through. This gives Liz hope, and motivation to never give up. Reading countless stories, ranging from these two authors and more, "it gave [her] a bigger imagination." An imagination to interpret her values, and generate more than just words on a page. But, but, but! Why write?

To different mindsets of people, writing is defined by various factors such as plot, moral of the story, characters, and so on. To Liz, she "[loves] how it gives [her] a chance to think like other people and be evil and play around with crazy situations." It grants her power. Freedom. Expression. She loves to be a puppeteer master. Waving words around with a magic wand, utilizing them not only for her own entertainment and stress relief, but for her reader's as well. Out of all the media forms, writing immediately yells, "Pick me!" to Liz, because "[she likes] getting the full story and plot of it all. [She loves] music and art and all, but instead of getting a fraction of the moment, [she likes] getting the whole thing." Not only does she get the whole shebang, "in the end, [she likes] seeing words on a paper and [having] the stories unravel." This is why Liz Nuno writes.

Pow! The reason why writing sticks out to her was a punch to my face. Expecting to dig deeper into my best friend's mind, I assumed I would know what she would say. Bam! Another smack to my face! I felt like Batman, endlessly being beaten up by his enemies. Expecting to learn that she wants to be an author and why she writes, I gained more of an appreciation for the reasoning and heart behind the answer, rather than the actual answer itself. It shocked me that I expanded my insight on my best friend. Who would have known that you can actually learn to know your best friend even more? I knew that she wanted to be an author and how she's "super" at writing, but I was clueless when it came to her thoughts about writing, and why she chose writing out of everything else. After talking with her, my jaw was to the floor. I was astonished to learn where her heart is, and how incredibly different writing is to individuals. She is truly passionate about this. And I cannot wait to be first in line to have her sign my copies of her books.

Look in the sky! It's a bird! It's a plane! It's not Super Man. It is Liz Nuno. Super Woman of writing stories. Nonetheless, a normal human being, destined to fight against the villains of writing as she moves her way up the ladder to become a top notch author. Even though she does not throw her fist down on a table declaring, "I want to be an author, and the best one," she knows that writing is a process. Heart and passion are deeply integrated into a career, and this girl has a lot of fiery passion and a singing soul. Writing definitely does not appeal to everyone. It is a unique taste bud that certain people need to fulfill. Like a garden. A magnificent garden. Some people favor the scent of the painting flower, or the music flower, or the movie flower, but not all people appreciate the writing flower. Liz Nuno is one of those people who, out of all the flowers, delicately plucked the gorgeous writing flower. She replants this flower in her own garden, so that one day, her flower can burst through the ground, extending leaf by leaf, until it stretches out and touches the bright blue sky. She truly has a wonderful gift, and nonetheless, a beautiful journey to fulfill her thirst for stories of her own.

Brianne St. Pierre is an animal science major.

Hope For The Lonely: You're Not Alone

Mac Hughes

Long brown hair, sparkling brown eyes, and always laughing. The kind of laugh that makes you smile even though you didn't hear the joke. She's a tiny thing, standing four feet and eleven inches tall. She's a self-proclaimed Hippie and does her best to live in love. We share everything from clothes and shoe size to the sound of our voices and laughs. We met in Kindergarten, over 13 years ago. To this day I'm not sure how we remained friends through all of her moves around the Bay Area; we were only in school together two years. I believe we were put in each other's lives for a reason; there is a greater purpose to our deep friendship and bond. Closer than a friend and more like a sister to me, she allows me to be a light in her life as much as she is one in mine. Her name is Hope.

Every day for the past 14 years of my existence she has allowed me to see my blessings, appreciate the little things, and never give up. You would never know by looking at her bright eyes and seemingly ever present smile that she was diagnosed with depression in sixth grade at the age of twelve and continues to struggle with this commonly misunderstood mental disorder every day. There are many things I never knew about her illness and life until I asked a few days ago. She doesn't want anyone's pity; she's too strong for her own good. She teaches me strength through her struggle, her experiences, and her willingness to carry on. We've convinced each other that we're never alone, we're capable of anything, and there's always a bright side to every situation. This is one of the many stories showing that people with depression aren't alone or don't have to be. This is the story of how our friendship saved Hope's life.

Nearly 20 million Americans "suffer from depression in any given year" (Murray). It has been around as long as humans have existed as we can see in biblical texts (Lanier 27). It is usually broken up and defined in three categories: "Major Depression, Dysthymia," or mild depression, and "Symptomatic Depression." Hope suffers from Major Depression, which is the most severe form causing "intense, incapacitating sadness" (Lanier 27). This means her depression follows her everywhere, and even when it isn't controlling her emotions it lingers in the back of her mind and causes her to have anxiety. Mild depression is a step down from Major Depression and is defined as being more long-term, but with less impairing, intense sadness. Symptomatic Depression is often called an "adjustment disorder" and is caused by a dramatic change in "normal" life, leaving one with a feeling of "low energy" (Lanier 27). These definitions are upsetting. They're so hopeless sounding; completely centered around sadness and gloom. These words do not define my best friend. It's important to recognize that there are ways to control depression. When I asked Hope if it had gotten easier for her to control her illness, she responded, "Absolutely, I'm getting more knowledgeable about it. I'm learning more and more tricks to get myself out of it sooner rather than later when it's full blown." Despite her ongoing wrestling with the most severe form of depression, she's taught herself to be the ruler of her body and fights to remain happy, healthy and in control. She began her fight by choosing optimism.

Helen Achat of Harvard's School of Public Health states, "An optimistic explanatory style is characterized by a belief that the future will be pleasant because one can control important outcomes" (Achat 127). Depression, in more than just Hope's case, leaves people feeling anxious, helpless and out of control. As I said before, even if the sadness isn't present, it is lurking.

Hope, however, expresses to me, "If I'm having a hard day, I'll remember a good event, place or person I love. I'll think 'it doesn't matter how sad I am right now because I know I can eventually get back to the happy point again.'" She is able to overpower and overcome the lurking sadness, anxiety and depression. She controls it using her optimism. She allows herself to be empowered by her sickness. Hope takes the challenge of depression and turns it into an energy source, allowing her to find reasons to stay positive. When I see her fighting depression I picture her a super hero. She is holding the negative energy of depression in her hand until she compresses it to create a ball of fire that she hurls down a dark tunnel to provide light to her path. She looks past the negative things her depression brings to the forefront and shoves them aside to see the light at the end of the tunnel; the good days to come. I've been honored to play a role in Hope's happiness. As her kindred spirit, my optimism, too, has often rubbed off on her.

LOOK HERE

If you or someone you know is struggling with depression or having difficulties dealing with the rigors of academic life, Cal Poly's Health and Counseling Services is here to help:
www.hcs.calpoly.edu/content/counseling/counseling-home

A little over a year ago, I gave Hope some very simple advice that I personally have always practiced. As I grew up and went through minor problems that seemed like the end of the world from my limited perspective on life, my mother, Kristy, would tell me to "count my blessings." She would say, "At first, you may want to feel sorry for yourself, but it's the quickest way to feel better." I passed this advice on to Hope, not thinking much of it. I give her advice all the time. It would be unusual for her to not reach out to me for help at least twice in any given month. I don't ever expect my advice to have such a great impact, but she recently expressed to me that she's continued to use this technique on a daily basis to allow herself to remain optimistic and looking towards the future. She tells me, "I always count the good, happy things in my life. It's honestly one of my favorite tools. I'll be so down and then I'll think, 'Well, at least I got that new pair of shoes, and I love my mom and she loves me, and I could be starving to death or not have running, clean water . . .' and so on, until I've warmed up my heart and outlook. It always lets me see the best in my day and realize things could easily be worse." This acts as a reminder that even though we may think nothing we say is helping, it is, and it's critical that we believe it does!

It has been found that "good relationships with" friends, "careers, teachers, co-workers and a supportive social network" allow "physical and emotional healing, happiness and life satisfaction, and prevents isolation and loneliness, major factors in depressive illness" (Murray). We have the ability to help. What it comes down to is the question of are we strong enough to help? Are we confident enough to love someone who needs us?

We should put aside our doubts and be confident, especially when this confidence can end up saving someone's life. A study performed by Petra Symister and Ronald Friend on the Influence of Social Support on Optimism in Depression found that "social support was important not only for reducing depression but also for increasing optimism." We should be outgoing and have self-esteem enough to raise others up and put a smile on their faces. I believe that our purpose on earth is to bring light and joy to others. When I asked Hope what makes her happiest, she simply responded, "Happy people, my family and friends. Something as simple as a smile can change the way I'm feeling." We should never be afraid to reach out and help. We've grown up with the phrase "put others before yourself," but it is time for us to start living by it. There are lives at stake and when something as simple as a smile or an open ear can provide a safety net, we should have no doubts! Our love and optimism can provide a friendship, a safe haven to those engaged in this ongoing fight. With confidence and a skip in our step, we have transformed ourselves into something no doctor could prescribe. Depression isn't something people wear around their neck. It is hidden in the minds of those who deal with it.

I never even knew Hope was diagnosed at such a young age until I asked her a few days ago. She is like a sister to me, and I never knew. It turns out that two thirds of those who suffer from depression do not seek treatment (Lanier 27). Those who are on the verge of darkness aren't willing to admit it or even to show signs of it. We live in a society where sadness equals weakness and asking for help is a sign of dependency. Bob Murray (PhD) states that "54 percent of people believe depression is a personal weakness." It takes strength, in this world, to admit you need help. It won't be obvious when someone needs us, so we should be quick to smile and make the time to listen without judgment. Someone who deals with depression is predisposed to a lack of social support (Symister 123). The largest knife depression holds to the throat of its bodies is loneliness. Depression brings mavericks of emptiness and isolation. Someone may be intentionally separating themselves because what used to bring them joy has been blackened by depression. Imagine the impact a smile, a welcoming, genuine "good to see you" or "how are you," can have on someone who is overcome with loneliness. You are blatantly showing them they are not alone. As effective as optimism is in battling depression, it sometimes gets in the way by blinding us to the affects depression has on the body.

When we were younger and Hope was first diagnosed with depression, I didn't understand. I felt it was an issue of mind over matter, essentially. I couldn't understand what she could possibly be so upset about. I would wish she could just get over it. I couldn't fathom the idea that someone's happiness was out of their hands. I've always been an optimist, believing that everything that happens in my life is under my control. Depression, however, is like any other disease; the sufferer doesn't have a choice. In his article on depression Eric Lanier says, "It affects how you feel, think, eat, sleep and act" (27). It's nothing to be taken lightly, it is a diagnosis, just like cancer or heart disease; it impairs the life of the body it lives in. It can even undermine the confidence of its host by lowering self-esteem (Symister 123).

The simplest way to increase self-esteem is to provide support (Symister 123). Being a happy confident person is one hundred percent correlated to the kinds of people you surround yourself with. Choose to be around supportive, loving people. Choose to smile when you feel the depression sucking the last drop of confidence from your skin. Don't allow this illness to control you. You are the master of your life. As Hope has shown, you can come from the worst of circumstances: hereditary depression, teen parents, a deaf and mentally impaired sister, constant moving from community to community and school to school and a lack of material resources, yet remain optimistic. What it takes is a positive outlook and a smile to fight through, to see the light at the end of the tunnel and refuse to give in to depression. Who knew such great inspiration could come in a package so tiny? She continues to amaze me. She continues, on a daily basis, to deny depression the right to define who she is. She has shown all of us that the difficult act of refusing to see the glass as half empty can have a profoundly positive effect on her illness.

We should never see the "diagnosed" as weak, incapable, pitiful people. We should love everyone, always. We should never believe we have learned everything there is to learn on any subject. Life's biggest lessons can come in the most unexpected forms. We should look to those struggling as heavy-weight champions of life. They are coping with things we may never understand. They are fighters. They are masters of confidence, friendship, happiness and optimism. They are the light at the end of the tunnel. They are inspiration. They are amazing, beautiful and abundantly, ridiculously and impressively strong. They are never alone. They are Hope.

Mac Hughes is a business major.

WORKS CITED

Achat, Helen, et al. "Optimism and Depression as Predictors of Physical and Mental Health Functioning: The Normative Aging Study." *Annals of Behavioral Medicine* 22.2 (2000): 127-30. Web. 12 May 2012.

Lanier, Eric. "Depression." *Professional Safety* (2003): 27-30. Web. 12 May 2012.

Levine-Mickel, Hope J. "Depression." Telephone interview. 14 May 2012.

Murray, Bob. "Depression Fact Sheet: Depression Statistics and Depression Causes." Uplift Program, 15 Jan. 2005. Web. 10 May 2012. <http://www.upliftprogram.com/>.

Symister, Petra and Friend, Ronald. "The Influence of Social Support and Problematic Support on Optimism and Depression in Chronic Illness: A Prospective Study Evaluating Self-Esteem as a Mediator." *Health Psychology* 22.2 (2003): 123-29. Web. 12 May 2012.

CONSIDER THIS

- *The writer uses positive and upbeat terms to describe her profile subject in the essay's introduction. What tone does this description set for the essay? Does Hughes want the reader to see Hope in a certain way? Does Hughes's viewpoint shift as the essay progresses? In other words, does the depiction of Hope become more complex?*
- *Hughes uses several sources to explain the clinical details of depression. How do these details add to the reader's understanding of Hope's experience? Do these sources add to the writer's credibility (ethos)? How can research help develop the focus and angle of your profile?*

Her Place in History

Roxanne Raye

The woman I know has a face of wrinkles that fold into her cheeks and crinkle at her eyes when she smiles. She loves hand knitted sweaters, sequined denim jackets and anything with a cat on it. Traditional, but never stuck in the past, she's the kind to stop picking vegetables from her home grown garden to squeeze me tight in a hug, then ask about how to work her new computer without missing a beat. Before I can even begin asking my questions on her life growing up during the war, a picture I found in my family's storage room some time ago pops up in my head. Back then she was a pale skinned girl with scrawny limbs and a short cut bob of light brown hair. As a farmer's daughter and the sister to a gaggle of brothers, she was often dirty and fulfilled the classic definition of a tomboy. To her, war is just another event in the long timeline of her life and perhaps not even the most dramatic or tragic of events, from her point of view. Still, there is importance in the fact that those small events and the specific details within our memories can impact us just as intensely as large ones.

At some point everyone learns about the World Wars that each rattled Europe to its core (if you didn't, shame on your history teachers). My grandmother on my father's side, Joy Soiseth Raye, grew up on a North Dakota farm during World War II. She was three years old at its beginning. When I called her up and asked how life on the farm was she responded with a bark of laughter and a single word, "Boring." I couldn't help but laugh along; I've always admired her honesty, it's something I feel I don't see enough of these days. "Dad and the boys never got drafted so I suppose that was a plus," she continued after a moment. "Everyone who was too chicken to fight wanted to be a farmer those days. Only time I ever remember someone saying they *wanted* to be a farmer." The touch of sarcasm and exasperation in her words told me she was probably rolling her eyes at the idea. Farming involves a great amount of hard, physical labor and, combined with the harsh seasons of North Dakota, I can't imagine it being high on anyone's career list.

Despite my misgivings, I pressed on, determined to discover something fantastic about living in the middle of nowhere during a huge war. I knew that questions about the war were traditionally geared towards people who lived in large cities or actually participated in the fighting, so I switched my tactics and simply asked, "What do you remember most about the war?" The voice on the other end of the line went silent, nearly one minute passing before she finally answered. "I remember being carefree and anxious at the same time. I wanted to know, but I didn't understand. I was so young when the war began, but in a way it shaped my life. It was so long ago, but there are some things I could never forget."

LOOK HERE

Examine the persuasive power of WWII posters with The National Archive's online exhibit of vintage visual rhetoric: www.archives.gov/exhibits/powers_of_persuasion/powers_of_persuasion_intro.html

It is hard for a child to truly grasp the concept of war since it involves so many heavy elements such as politics, the economy and death. The last one sticks the most vividly for it is the most violent and logically frightening thing. Joy talked about listening to the radio with her family; they always had it on and there were only a couple of channels that came through clear enough to sort between. She didn't know what they were talking about most of the time, but she didn't need to. Just the uncertainty in the voices of the radio hosts, the shifts from frantic to depressed, were enough to build up a little bubble of anxiety in the back of her mind. "It really didn't become real until I went to the movie theater," she told me. It took me a moment to skip through my memories from history class to remember that sometimes before movies or between double features they would play news reels of the war, most of it propaganda. I was brought out of my thoughts as she continued, "All I remember about the news was that there were lot of explosions and gunfire, I was so scared my aunt took me home before the movie started. I never got to see *Snow White*."

The details in this little memory stuck out to me. My grandmother was not distraught about the more horrific images of the war she vaguely remembered, but instead recalled sadly about never getting to see Disney's first animated movie. What stuck out is that I can relate to little details on a personal level. I don't have a vivid mental picture of the Twin Towers crumpling to the ground in New York, but I do remember being pulled aside at the airport as officials did an in depth search of my bag. I don't remember where I was going or what for, just my heart beating faster and tears welling up in my eyes. Now that I'm older such an event would be an annoyance, but as a child, being singled out because a McDonald's toy in my carry on looked funny in the scan was absolutely terrifying.

Without asking directly, I listened for more little insights that at some other time may have been brushed off. I didn't have to wait long. She described to me the letters her uncles sent to her while they fought overseas. Along with other history geeks, I loved to hear about how the letters came back with little phrases and words crossed out, evidence of censorship by high officials, but at the same time I forced myself to ignore it and focus on why she remembered the event so well. "Uncle Mags would send a piece or two of gum in his letters," she recounted in a tone that told me she had a smile on her face. A smile grew on my face as well. Gum, such a simple thing, almost trivial, but that is what she remembered. I asked why and replied with another light chuckle, "You know how kids are. We loved candy." And I did know. After all, I vividly remember a substitute teacher in elementary school simply because he gave out gummy bears for correct answers.

Finally I decided to voice a question that had been slowly growing inside me throughout the interview: if the war did not directly affect her childhood, how did it affect her adult life? For this question I received a sigh and a quiet, "It made me thankful." My grandmother is referring to the fact that her family did not lose her uncles to the war and didn't have to fear the draft or air raids. "I remember Bob telling me how he had to hide with Sophie at night when the sirens went off," she explained, referring to my grandfather and his mother. My grandmother's husband grew up on at the beach in southern California, just outside of Los Angeles. With the threat of Japanese air strikes, nightly blackouts were never optional. Another small laugh, but this time melancholy with memories, "I wish he was still here to tell you about that, it was much more interesting I think." War is never easy, though its reality hinders some more than others. My grandmother may not believe her story was that interesting, but I do. Among the stories of terror and politics, the story of a simple home life such as hers is often left untold.

Saying our goodbyes, I reviewed the interview in its entirety. I called my grandmother expecting stories about WWII, dramatic stories about how it affected her home town and the country as a whole. But what I received instead was the understanding that not everything those days revolved around the war, despite what the history books tell you. To my grandmother, details that are rather useless to a historian are key components in her memories as an individual. Her place in history was defined by moments, just as I think all of our lives are. You can say, 'I grew up during a war,' but that means nothing unless you can explain how that experience affected your life.

Roxanne Raye is a manufacturing engineering major.

WORK CITED

Raye, Joy Soiseth. Phone Interview. 21 Oct. 2011.

CONSIDER THIS

- *As she conveys her grandmother's memory of not seeing* Snow White, *Raye connects the moment to her own recollection of 9/11. How do these stories relate to each other? What do they say about the civilian experience in war?*
- *The writer uses WWII to focus her essay. How does this angle affect the essay as a whole? Do we learn more about her grandmother as a person? How does the writer use anecdotes to maintain this focus?*
- *An effective profile strikes a balance between the writer's and subject's voices. Does this profile essay strike that balance? In other words, does it feel like Raye's grandmother is speaking* with *her in this essay—and not* for *her?*

Homeless Not Hopeless

Ariana Montes

Raindrops are gently falling from the cloud-bearing sky. I peek through my fogged-up window and find exactly what I am looking for. Sitting under the only sheltered part of the bus stop is an old man with layers upon layers of ragged and torn clothing. I park my car and start the short walk to him with umbrella in hand. As I get closer, I am able to notice much more than I had at first glance. From head to toe, he appears, for lack of a better term, old. He looks up at me and I instantly smile due to my genuine excitement in finding the right person. My introduction and invitation to lunch lead to his nod of approval and acceptance. We awkwardly walk side by side towards Chipotle. It is in this moment that I am completely unaware of what I am getting myself into. I didn't know it yet, but this lunch would end up teaching me much more about what is really important in life.

Carl Haynes was born in Melstone, Montana. He was the only child born to a farm working couple. As a young child, he was forced to witness the loss of his home, the loss of that wide front yard that he used to run forever in, and most importantly, the loss of his parents—all because of a common drug known as methamphetamine. By the time he reached high school, Carl decided that he was fed up with having nearly everything in life being taken away from him. He dropped out of high school his sophomore year after overhearing incessant chatter from some friends about how construction jobs were abundant in California. Optimistic about this opportunity, Carl packed up what was left of his possessions and headed to Redding, California where jobs were indeed abundant. The problem, however, was that the jobs were not as stable as he had hoped. There were times when he had jobs and money, but other times where both were insufficient. Because of this, he decided to hitchhike with some other men down south in pursuit of more stable work opportunities.

Before finally ending up in San Luis Obispo, Carl had his share of dealing with mean people. He sadly recalls a time where a woman came up to him with her young boy in her arms. She stood directly in front of Carl and pointed at him with an insulting finger. With clear disregard for any of his feelings or background, she told her young son that if he did not go to school, he would end up with a horrible life like the bum in front of them. While I listened to Carl recall this terrible situation, his demeanor showed internal pain. Situations similar to this one are very common for Carl. Throughout all of his hardships, however, Carl remained positive and optimistic, hopeful that he would eventually find peace.

It was not until he ended up in San Luis Obispo County that Carl found a place he could call home. He instantly felt much more welcomed than in any town before, which became clear after he declared, "The people here are just so much nicer." His feelings on the matter were evident as he spoke about instances where people showed generosity by either handing money to him or simply flashing a smile. He spoke about how the town as a whole is a "much happier" one. When I asked him what he meant by this, he calmly explained, "You know when you're in a sad mood and all it takes is one person to smile at you? Yeah, that's the kinda feelin' I get around here, but it's always from more than one person." As touching as this is, I asked Carl to give me an example of someone being nice to him. He happily spoke to me about how a man in a business suit, appearing "too professional to be wanting to talk to a homeless person", once came up to him and told him that he should find a way to go the El Camino Homeless Organization (ECHO) in Atascadero. This man stood there for a few minutes and talked to Carl about how he often volunteers with his family at ECHO and how he watches homeless men and women happily eat fulfilling meals and make friends. Thanks to that man's information, Carl now visits the shelter once in a while when desperate situations arise and he cannot find means to get food. Carl gave me insight to the organization and what they do, and actually influenced my decision to do a volunteer project there.

LOOK HERE

To learn more about the El Camino Homeless Organization, or to volunteer, visit http://www.echoshelter.net/

In an attempt to further my knowledge of people in SLO County, I asked Carl what the nicest thing anybody has ever done for him was. He explained how when he first got to SLO, it was a rainy day and he was cold and miserable sitting outside of CVS, when a lady went into the store and came out with a brand new umbrella and a thick, warm blanket. He could not believe his eyes when she walked up and gave them both to him. He actually recalls this situation being the main reason he decided to stay in this area. As he finished this story about a woman's compassion, Carl stated, "And you're a fool if you don't mention that what you did for me today is at the top of the list right next to that nice lady who gave me the blanket and umbrella." He made it clear that by me treating him to lunch and getting his story down on paper, he felt like he finally was making a difference in this world. He spoke to me about how although he knows he has a kind heart; he also knows that he has made no attribution to the community by being homeless. With my help of getting his story down on paper, "even if only four people read it," Carl has left an impact. I can attest to this because Carl really did make an impact on me. I have always been curious, yet have never gone out of my way to understand that there may be much more to a homeless person than meets the eye. I know now that this is completely true.

After spending time learning about Carl's life, I gained insight to what is really important to him. It was hard for me to initially understand how he could have such a huge smile on his face even though he had been through so many misfortunes, and ultimately ended up living on the street. I was quickly enlightened after I asked him about this and heard—with much enthusiasm—"I get to sit around all day and watch people be mad and not know how god-damn lucky they are, you know?" Taking it into perspective, it is easy to see why Carl feels this way. People do not appreciate the little things in life anymore. They get stuck in the hustle and bustle of everyday life and forget what is truly important. Carl is fortunate in the sense that because he does not have tangible luxuries, he is able to appreciate what really matters in life.

Taking a step back and reflecting on my interview with Carl reminds me how important it is to appreciate what I have. By eliminating all of the unnecessary luxuries from my life, I can picture how life would be so different; yet if I think about it, I would still have what is most important. I would still have my family, which is the priority of my importance, my friends, and my open heart. It is with these three things that I find true happiness—I would not need anything else in the world other than these. Having so many luxuries sometimes gets in the way of remembering the three things that are most important to me.

Carl has nothing though. This would appear to be the situation to any naked eye. I was even guilty of the thought before actually speaking with him. What I learned throughout my interview, however, is that Carl is happy because he has more than the people around him. He may not have the newest iPhone, or anything with a high value of money for that matter, but what he does have is much deeper than those materialistic items—he has an open mind and an open heart. This is obvious to me after hearing him speak with such a warm heart about his experiences. With these, he is able to delve far past the things that do not matter. Although he does not have a family, nor does he have a stable living situation, Carl gained my utmost respect because of how happy he is. Through talking to him, I am now able to see through his eyes and take a step back to appreciate the innate luxuries that I am blessed with.

Ariana Montes is a statistics major.

WORK CITED

Haynes, Carl. Personal Interview. 27 April 2012.

CONSIDER THIS

- *In this profile, the author offers a fair amount of introspection; she uses the information obtained from the interview to examine her own views on life and luxury. Does she effectively balance her own voice with that of the interviewee? Ultimately, who or what does this profile depict?*
- *This essay uses several direct quotations from the interview. What do these quotations add to the profile? Do they seem fully integrated into the text itself? In other words, do they both enrich the content and improve the flow of the essay?*

The Start of Pee Water Springs

Pee Water Season

Bo Ellis

"Tradition" is a word I hear a lot, whether that be celebrating a holiday such as Easter, or singing happy birthday to a loved one. For whatever the cause, I feel as though tradition brings everyone together and reminds us why we practice such a gathering in the first place. When I think of summer I think of all the aspects as to what makes it a traditional summer such as, beach days, late nights, and no school. If asked the same question around a group of my friends a unanimous answer of "Pee Water Run!" would be expected. The Pee Water Run is simply a tradition. It started out one summer in 8th grade, while on a walk to the beach with my two friends. We always had to walk around this canyon, which we found very annoying. One day we decided to no longer walk around the canyon, but go through it. My friends and I faced challenging obstacles, which reminded us of the show *Man vs. Wild* with Bear Grylls. We loved this guy and tried to make a simple trail feel as though we were lost in a dense Amazon rain forest. My friends and I made it to the ocean exhausted, beat up, and thrilled from navigating the maze we just accomplished. We did not learn until later that this journey we defeated would bring us back year after year, allowing us to reunite, bond, and continue a great tradition.

Pee Water Springs is as nasty as it sounds, rapid flowing sewer water along with urban runoff channeling its way down the canyon making the trail. One of my friends, Will Peterson, was terrified of the water: "I did not know what to call it on my first run, it smelled like sewer water, or pee. Well whatever it was, I was not going to touch it." Pee Water Springs is different; even though it may have a rough exterior, when I take a step back to reel in all of its natural beauty, I realize just how special this place is. While a flowing stream of pee water may sound disgusting, in reality, the stream feeds the life around it; turning a river of pee into a beautiful array of plants we like to think of as our own jungle.

LOOK HERE

San Luis Obispo has excellent hiking trails. To see a map of the area's trails, visit this site:
http://visitslo.com/cm/Activities/HikeSLO.html

I look at my friends that demonstrate a rough exterior, a thick leathery skin that cannot be broken into. The run changes this between my friends and me. The trail breaks down all restrictions that my friends express on the outside and allows us to open up and feel for each other. My friend Owen describes how the run brings us together, "By doing the Pee Water Run we can ensure that homies will be homies and will stay homies; there is a bond formed and all walls can be broken down; everyone cares for each other." It really is a magical time, as the hard surface radiating from my friends disintegrates so that we all can look past what makes us tough. I began to realize that my pals are going through struggles and need a buddy there to lean on. I love this about my friends, whatever the circumstances we can be serious with one another and support each other in hard times. The trail is tough and rugged, just like my friends. Opening up the trail and the feelings of my friends reminds us of how we care for one another; it turns a hard obstacle into a powerful setting for real truth to be said, and real connections to be made.

All of my buddies felt that the Pee Water Run was a time to re-group and reconnect with one another. When our gang all left for college, staying connected was harder than expected. Will Peterson described the Pee Water Run as a tradition as to how we regroup. "The Pee Water run symbolizes a tradition that, although is ridiculous and half the time half the people get poison oak, we all can come back and talk about ten years later." Trying to all stay in touch through *facebook* and other social networking sites does not work amongst my friends. This is why we need to regroup for the Pee Water Run every year; not only does it bring us together for an awesome experience, but it actually gets my friends and I face to face. Owen Franco, a veteran in the season and my partner on the first ever Pee Water Run said, "3 days is enough time to get in touch with everyone, by the time the day comes everyone is too stoked to forget about such an occasion." This run brings my best friends back to reality rejuvenating the group, all excited to reconnect, talk about our lives, and enjoy the time we spend every year together engaging in the Pee Water Run. I hear and learn more about what my friends have done in the past 3 months of their lives in one day at Pee Water Springs than most people should hear about their friends in a lifetime. Having the same group of friends really grants us to trust each other and have each other's backs.

Throughout our trials on the trail, I learned that good friends really have support for one another, a main reason we can get through obstacles presented. Timo Ingram another one of my best friends detailed that one of his strongest feelings on the trail is the support our group has for each other. Timo recalls:

> One of my more fond moments was in one of the earlier runs and it was in an early section of the run where we had to jump up the steep dirt wall and it kept getting sketchier after each guy went. By the end it was a full on team effort helping the last few guys up and that was fuckin' awesome, like war shit, like "come on men!!!!!!" haha.

I remember the dirt wall: tall, barren, and a slide I did not want to fall down. This bluff had gotten so steep and overused that the foot holders to climb were nothing more than a slick step strait down into the dreadful pee water. To get beyond this my friends had to trust in one another and work as a unit to complete.

A ruthless group indeed, nothing stopped my friends, so we continued to climb. We soon realized the only way up was to get pulled. It got to the point that friends were jumping up this hill, missing the top, and then having to maneuver like a ninja to get back to the other side without touching the pee water. It felt just like a movie when two people are locking hands from a helicopter after an explosion and getting pulled up to safety. I had made it across this dirt hill and still had to pull friends up; I could not do this task alone. My remaining buddies on top of the dirt face would have to pull up our fellow brother with every bit of energy we had. My friends and I were so strong together, had such great teamwork that this mission turned into nothing but a mere task. We concluded this task together and all laid on the edge of that dirt face laughing at what we just did. I can also relate to Timo as climbing being one of my most fond memories. The power of friends and the power of teamwork is something that should be felt by all. This is one of the most sobering feelings to have to go through, and it is definitely one that I will never forget. Things get pretty hairy on the trail; however, about half way through is where we meet the real challenge.

Tucked away from plain view, the landmark my friends dubbed the "Leap of Faith," is surrounded by a wilderness of green trees as well as native California shrub. This Leap restricts us from one side of the trail to the other; without the hurdle there is nowhere to go but back. Standing vertically at 20 feet and horizontally at 15, the jump is not the worst part. My buddies all love the leap; however, our parents do not. One of the best thrills when returning to the trail and leap is the fact that one of your friends is going down. On the past 3 occasions there has been difficulties resulting in rallying and helping our friends out of the trail. One in particular was of Harrison, he was last to jump and was also his first time; first timers don't do well. My friends and I were all behind him while he took his jump, he trusted us. Gearing up, running, and taking the lurch my buddies and I knew he was in for it. Harrison broke his ankle, and we freaked out. Friends were screaming, others were laughing, but we were all together. We were the best of friends, all behind each other; we just conquered this jump and were going to carry Harrison out. Put into a sticky situation, my buddies all had trust and love for another, and would do anything to help each other out. Events like this do not disappear; a true feeling of trust and dependence was mutual amongst my buds.

We have returned many times to the Pee Water Run as well as the Leap of Faith and each time it is a different obstacle. This trail is more than just a jump it's a time to rebuild. My friends and I carried on the tradition all throughout high school and added new members along the way. The Trail has changed since the first attempt, but so have my friends. The Pee Water Run is more than a trail it's a time to rejoin with the best of buds, to catch up. The leap is a reality check, no matter how old we become one thing stays the same; we need to cross this jump and, we need to do it together. The Leap of Faith along with the trail not only challenges me to be brave, but also is a place where I know I can go back and still have the same group of friends the first time journeying through. The trail is there to show that no matter how hard the obstacle, it can be overcome. It shows that no matter what happens good friends will take that jump with you.

Bo Ellis is an agribusiness major.

WORKS CITED

Ellis, Bo. "The Start of Pee Water Springs." Personal Photo 22 July. 2011.

Franco, Owen. Personal Interview. 4 April. 2012.

Ingram, Timo. Online Interview. 6 April. 2012.

Peterson, Will. Personal Interview. 4 April. 2012.

CONSIDER THIS

- *Defining an essay's key terms helps the reader better understand the author's ideas. For instance, in Ellis's essay, he defines what the word "tradition" means to him and his friends. What is your definition of "tradition?" How do "traditions" help sustain relationships?*
- *Ellis profiles a place, but he uses narrative and description to help develop his thesis. How does this strategy help the audience connect to the author's recollections?*
- *Ellis conducted multiple interviews for his essay. How do the multiple perspectives develop his profile of this space?*

"AND THEN OUR MAN, MR DE JAGER, TOLD THE PRESIDENT …"

Jurgen de Jager

The old wooden turntable stealing the silence with wonderful Johnny Cash blues reminds him of an adventurous youth. The 25-year old Brandy he retrieves from the cellar reminds him of the company he has kept over the years. The worn in family Bible proudly resting on the coffee table—He remembers being a believer, a man of God and how it changed his life. There is culture and history engraved in these walls. Paintings by Pierneef and other well-known artists decorate the rooms. Together with antique Persian carpets, it completes the setting. His black and white framed photographs, each telling a different story: stories of his chess matches against the former President (then called Prime Minister), his differences with the Broederdond and struggle with the 'Apartheid Government.' Stories of dining with English royalty or the time he travelled 600 miles by foot, herding 900 cattle across the country to find better grazing. Hennie Petrus de Jager is my grandfather and he knows about change …

I enter the room with two drinks. The ice in his drink bumps against the glass. It sounds like music whenever he takes a small sip. I look down at the drink in my hand and I gaze across the deep, opaque plum-black appearance and wonder what kind of wonderful flavors lurk beneath—much like when I look at my grandfather. I take a sip of the 2004 Meerlust Cabernet Sauvignon and sit down. The palate is full yet elegant and finishes with a lingering dark fruit flavors. I can always judge a man on what kind of wine he gives me.

"Thank you my boy," he says after taking his first sip "It's just the way I like it." I smile and acknowledge the compliment. "It's a good thing I've been practicing. Dad also enjoys a drink after work every now and then." My reply is met by a chuckle, his legendary chuckle. After a few minutes discussing current news events, the weather, and the fix on all sporting events, we move onto some deeper thoughts. We start speaking about his early days and what impact it had on his future. He briefly leaves the conversation to get a few pictures to substantiate his (already convincing) story. He returns to the room with a more business like expression—He makes his way to the seat and gives me a gentle nod. My cue to continue. "Grandfather, please tell me about your childhood." He sits back and crosses his legs. Silence, and another small sip.

"I was born on a small farm in South Africa in 1929. I was one of five children," I could gather by the increased empathy in his voice that he had a fond childhood—the old photos substantiate my assumption. "I graduated from high school in 1946, and due to financial constraints, was unable to attend college." "I imagine that had to be a set back?" "Indeed it was," he replies "The trick is to never stop trying—a year later I got a job at Volkskas, a major South African bank. This gave me time and money to further my studies." The way he conducts this interview relates to the way he approaches most things in life—methodical, in order and always diligent.

This was the first time my grandfather spoke to me about his beginnings and like most good men, he came from humble beginnings. It was difficult to imagine him as a young man working his way through life—I had this fixed image of him with his silver grey hair and old golden-framed glasses, always reserved. However, I enjoyed learning about his younger side and I could relate to it on some levels. His hardworking and honest youth laid a strong foundation. It gave his adventurous spirit some structure—enabling him to put his entrepreneurial skills to good use.

"After 10 years at the bank, I identified an opportunity to become an equal partner in a plant that specialized in the manufacturing of agricultural machinery and equipment", He slips out a smile and continues. "Over the next 12 years the company experienced rapid growth and was sold to a large corporate agricultural group." I realize in the silence that there was a reason for his satisfying smile. A smile almost suggesting that 'a plan' came together. I was eager to find out more. "What did you do with the monies you received?" "I hope he left some for me!" I hear my dad shout from the window. I can't help but join in the laughter . . . and my grandfather's chuckle. "The extra funds enabled me to purchase farmlands—which ultimately got me involved in corn farming, and that opened up an exciting and important new chapter in my life."

I was keen to ask my next question but before I could, my father now made his way onto the patio and rested his strong right hand on my shoulder and said: "I bet you don't know that some years ago your grandfather met with the President." I nod my head but only realize what he just said a few seconds later. "The President of what?" I ask, "The President of our country" my grandfather now replies—way too casually for my liking. "Why, about what?" I ask a bit dumbfounded. "We were discussing some important matters at the time, and we played some chess, you know the usual." This is far from usual I think to myself. "What kind of matters where you discussing?" The blunt questions just keeps coming, I can't help it. "In those days, corn farming provided a poverty stricken country with cheap, good quality food. It was a massive industry, and played a pivotal role in South Africa—the staple food to the 'masses'. This caused some people to take advantage of the booming industry and some forms of manipulation were taking place. At the time I was one of the biggest corn farmers in the country." I see a smile creep up on his face "Not literally the biggest—you know what I mean ha-ha."

His sense of humor always snuck up on me. He has a sharp wit and a way of brightening a conversation. There's almost a sense of innocence in his humor, but in his stories he usually only means business. "The President and I made use of the opportunity to also discuss matters regarding the corn industry, and seeing that I was one of the leaders of the group that rebelled against the agricultural union, we both knew that the 'corn-topic' cannot be ignored for too long." He picks up his drink. The music is still there, almost like a prelude to what is coming next. "Was he angry? What did he say?" I ask, with a little bit too much enthusiasm. "It was tough and to the point discussions. The struggle between our organization and the Government backed agricultural union lasted 14 years."

LOOK HERE

To learn more about the farm workers union:
http://www.ufw.org/

He takes out a few pictures and newspaper articles—and shows me some examples of the conflicts. He points to a specific edition. It's him on the front page of the Sunday newspaper. This is going to be interesting! The reserved, frail look now departs and makes way—I start envisioning my grandfather as a leader, and revolutionary who brought about positive change. Not just changes he experienced, but also the changes he brought on others and it was always changes for the better.

I enjoy the contrasts as he continues his story "In the mid and late 1960s there was a growing unhappiness amongst corn farmers. Government, through the South African Agricultural

Union (SAAU) and the Maize Board had, since the early 1840s, a single-channel marketing system for determining corn prices. Prices were 'fixed' by a small group of people, always in the interest of Government. Farmers were increasingly dissatisfied with the methods, and results, of price determination and the controlled use of the Stabilization Fund. This lead to a divide between farmers, small scale and industrial, and confrontation with agricultural unions, co-operatives and the Government."

Silence follows as my grandfather takes a long gaze into the stars, gathering his thoughts. The image reminds me of a famous Nietzsche quote: "When you look into an abyss, the abyss also looks into you."—I conclude that this has to be the reason for the stars in his eyes.

With his two stars now firmly fixed on me, he continues. "I was a large scale farmer,—one of the 20% of corn farmers that accounted for 80% of the country's corn production. When decisions needed to be made at SAAU and Maize Board level, votes (and decisions) were based on numbers, and not production levels. This inevitably led to a policy that was not in the long term interest of farmers, or sustained corn production in the country in general." Fact for fact and piece by piece this brilliant puzzle started showing me glimpses of the complete picture. "Is this where SAMPI started?" I ask, hoping to find another piece. "Exactly!" he says "This ultimately caused the forming of an independent group called SAMPI (South African Maize Producers Institute) in 1970. I was a founder member and elected Chairman later on. In the prologue to establishing SAMPI, several attempts of dialogue were made, and after negotiations with leading members of the SAAU, the industrial farmers were 'branded' as arrogant for challenging age-old policy, and Government. Their actions were seen as attempting to divide the agricultural structures in place."

I was amazed by his attention to detail—to proud and honest to tweak any details, albeit insignificant. I was planning getting through a few more chapters, but I liked where this was going so I continued on this specific trail of discovery. The perfect ingredients for a book or a movie I think to myself. "What distinguished SAMPI from SAAU? And did you implement any changes?"

"The majority of the members of the SAAU were also members of a secret organization called the "Afrikaner Broederbond (AB) (similar to a brotherhood)", which later became infamous for their unfair manipulation of key administrative appointments (e.g. heads of universities, editors of newspapers, etc.) and apartheid policies. The influence of the AB extended into various departments of government, as they had the majority of members in the Cabinet." I wait for him to continue, but they only sound comes from the fresh ice cubicles in his drink. "Any changes?" I ask, thinking that he forgot about the second part of my question. "Oh ja!" he gasps "It must be the age my boy. There were definitely a few changes I wanted to implement. Our new constitution stipulated that office holders must express no political party affiliation and be subject to annual re-election. Three motifs were very important: 1) an autonomous organization, 2) specialized corn farmers and 3) democratically accountable to its member."

The SAAU, with the support of the powerful AB, set out to dismantle the newly formed SAMPI. The SAAU started experiencing financial difficulties, and used their AB ties in government to pass legislation in which all corn producers had to pay an annual levy to the SAAU. This legislation forced SAMPI supporters to contribute to the SAAU, who in essence was their enemy.

"The Government took many measures to try and nullify the existence of SAMPI. They even presented an official document to the army, declaring SAMPI as "Persona non Grata," which essentially ignores their existence."

History has showed that it is a bad idea to be on the Government's bad side, but this did not discourage my grandfather. After asking him how on earth he managed to overthrow such a deep rooted organization he told me of his brilliant plan : "The only way to ensure unity within the corn producing industry was to persuade the AB that a congress needed to be held—the so-called 'unity congress'. It was of key importance to SAMPI was that voting had to be based on production levels." My granddad knew that if they could persuade the AB, they will effectively force the SAAU to agree to the decision and join the congress.

This congress eventually took place in 1980, and through a democratic voting process, SAMPI successfully took control over the entire corn industry in South Africa. A new organization was founded, National Maize Producers Organization (NAMPO) and my grandfather was elected Vice-Chairman. In later years he also held the position of Chairman of NAMPO and the South African Maize Board, where he was a key role player in high level international marketing. This position gave him the opportunity to travel all across the world, including countries like Japan, Korea, Romania, Taiwan and Europe.

LOOK HERE

For more information about NAMPO:
http://www.grainsa.co.za/nam_index.php

My grandfather currently resides on his Game Farm—Wilton Valley—and spends his days with his family, accommodating hunters—and with surplus funds, he establishes new animal species on the farm and helps sustain the small village neighboring his farm. The stories he told, and the thoughts he shared inspired my newfound inspired outlook. I always enjoy when my dad draws comparisons between me and my grandfather, the cross legged sitting or maybe our shared interest of the outdoors. Like listening to the music as he slowly sips his drink—he taught me to find joy in the delicate things in life.

Jurgen de Jager is an economics major.

CONSIDER THIS

- *De Jager not only offers a portrait of his grandfather today, but he also dives into his grandfather's past to better understand his "beginnings." In short, the essay covers quite a bit of territory. Did de Jager effectively transition between different moments in his grandfather's rich life?*
- *Examine the details and descriptive moments in de Jager's essay. For example he writes, "I look down at the drink in my hand, and I gaze across the deep, opaque plum-black appearance and wonder what kind of wonderful flavors lurk beneath—much like when I look at my grandfather." How does this technique help develop the reader's understanding of de Jager's grandfather?*

Analysis

How does a text communicate with an audience?

Alone Time

[I took this image] while walking through the architecture building, another student walking alone stopped by this exhibit. The idea of solitude is amplified in this image by the white surrounding the student, making her seem even more "alone."

I was able to capture a sense of intrigue in the photo that can only be achieved when you have time to be alone and reflect on the things you appreciate. Assuming that the figure photographed in the image was an architecture student, it perfectly explains why spending time alone can help one with their passions. Examining the image more, the sculpture itself could be the girl's own creation; she could be admiring the work that she put into it. Being alone in this sense could mean one of calmness and having time to do things one enjoys, to spend time with one's passions, or to indulge in the things that one cannot every day.

David Jang took this photo and wrote this brief analysis. David is a forestry and natural resources major.

The 11th Hour: A Review

Caleb Knight

"Ah, refreshing, cold water—this reminds me of my home pond. I wonder if I'll ever get back there. I hope the new eggs are faring well. It seems like yesterday that I was hatched from my own egg, and started working at growing my legs and losing the tail. I believe it was the end of a summer—the water was still warm though. Quite like this water. This reminds me of a warm summer pond. Except the water in this small, silvery pond is very clear. There aren't any lily pads for lounging or flies for catching. I don't like this small pond, but at least the water is really warm. Perhaps it has grown warmer—it's hard to tell, but no worries, I'm relaxed. Yes this water is indeed hot—but it's nice. I'm cozy, and it's bearable. Perhaps I'll rest my eyes for a while—I haven't seen a bird in what seems like ages. I'll be safe for a short, floating nap."

Of course, when this frog decided to nap, the water in the pot he rested in was already close to boiling. Lulled into an illusion of safety by the gradual change of his surroundings, he would be cooked alive. Only a few decades ago, scientists began claiming that society is a frog in its own pot, slowly killing itself through climate change and global warming. What began as vague theories and ideas grew into a panicked, study-backed common realization of the state of our planet. Awareness was increased by figures like Al Gore and the United Nations Intergovernmental Panel on Climate Change (Bisland 1). They had summarized the problem, speaking of how man-made gases like excess carbon dioxide were accumulating in our atmosphere and causing what is known as a "greenhouse effect," in which trapped heat slowly raises the planet's temperature. It was in this nervous, stalled environment of 2007 that Leonardo DiCaprio produced his film *The 11th Hour*. This documentary effectively employs emotion-provoking scenes and music, as well as educated interview perspectives to increase awareness of our climate change crisis. The film argues that though our planet's current state is dire and not completely redeemable, it is salvageable through active environmentally-friendly measures on both an individual and worldwide scale.

The credibility of *The 11th Hour* is well established by the appearances of renowned experts and scientists, and the production of seasoned actor Leonardo DiCaprio. Critics would claim the extensive interviews are tedious and dry, but they contribute immensely to the ethos of the documentary. An audience leans forward and inclines their ears to the words of experts and experienced figures. Of course, too much leaning forward and ear inclining may eventually prove strenuously mundane, but for an issue of such importance as our planet's survival, my attention was maintained. Physicist Steven Hawking, former Soviet head Mikhail Gorbachev, former CIA head R. James Woosley Jr., and Nobel Prize winner Wangari Maathai are among the fifty well known experts and environmentalists who share in interviews throughout the film. Their perspectives were not merely spoken, however. Producer Leonardo DiCaprio backed almost every statement spoken with perfectly appropriate video evidence either captured by his crew, or collected from around the world. The documentary further flaunted DiCaprio's skill with specially timed scene placement, such as the shot of DiCaprio speaking in front of a large oak tree, relating the critical nature of the time, and the necessity of affirmative action. The oak tree, known for its resiliency through age, seems to be a symbol of hope in the film, strategically placed directly before the documentary shifts from illustrating the global warming crisis to proposing affirmative action for the future.

Many other scenes of *The 11th Hour* are infused with pathos in form of words and images, further strengthening the film's depiction of crisis, and its argument for environment-saving action on the personal and global scale. For example, the opening few minutes consist of images such as starving, hungry babies, crumbling icebergs, burning forests, and thick pollution. The second man of the film to speak claims our planet "is sick. We have a planet that's behaving like an infected organism." The fourth man makes similar statements, but places blame on humanity rather than simply stating the severity of our biosphere, saying that we as a race are "ultimately committing suicide." Instantly the viewer is hit with the gravity of the situation—an easy situation to recognize and understand from the images of real life. There are no actors, no set scenes, no computer graphics. Near the end of the documentary, DiCaprio stands on a cliff overlooking a vast blue ocean. He begins to speak of the critical time period that we are living in, and refers to the growing, world-unifying trend of environmentalism, saying our generation's strategic response to the damage caused by industrialized civilization could "very well save this unique blue planet for future generations." This inspirational speech creates emotions of hope and determination in the audience. Even the camera angle of this scene inspires hope for redemption. First it causes the viewers to understand that they stand with DiCaprio on a cliff along with humanity, flirting with the edge and teetering over self-extinction from climate change. Secondly the audience sees a pure, blurry blue landscape in the distance behind the speaker, causing them to realize that with the proper response he speaks of, the future may offer a renewed, beautiful world.

LOOK HERE

To see a trailer for The 11th Hour, *visit this site:*
http://topdocumentaryfilms.com/11th-hour/

The documentary uses logos in the organization of the core message, allowing its audience to first fully grasp the catastrophic issue before introducing hope with a call to action. Humanity cannot fight against an enemy they cannot fully see, so the beginning half of *The 11th Hour* consisted mostly of images of our "sick" world, and experts relating quantitatively the damage being done to Earth. Many specific statistics and careful studies are quoted. When encountered with such a direct threat to something the audience loves, like Earth's natural beauty and life for future generations, viewers are logically led to asking, "What can we do about it?" Awareness of such a worldwide issue without an action plan would leave viewers despondently defeatist. Producer DiCaprio planned for this response by saving proposals for action until nearer to the end of the film. Ultimately, the call to action is summarized by Paul Hawken in the film, when he says society needs to "reimagine every single thing we do. There isn't one single [thing] that we make or systems that we have that doesn't require a complete re-make." Examples of this logical conclusion are given in form of alternate power sources, new architectural designs, and mimicry of nature's systems for human systems. Personal choices are also emphasized for their importance, as well as governmental policy. Within a short year after the release of *The 11th Hour*, many people who followed the argument from crisis-awareness to action published articles relating their ideas, such as Bryan Walsh of *Time* magazine. Walsh proposes changes such as a national charge on carbon emissions, "coupled with tougher energy-efficiency mandates and significant new public and private investment in green technologies" (7). As illustrated by both *The 11th Hour* and Walsh's article published in the next year, logical organization is essential for an effective argument—first clearly defining the crisis, and proposing ideas for action secondly.

Surprisingly, despite overwhelming evidence, there are still voices in society who shout in opposition to the basic arguments of *The 11th Hour*. Columnist Patrick Buchanan of *Human Events* is one prominent voice claiming global warming is a hoax, and the illusion of crisis was developed to make a unified yet truly ignorant world that is more willing to be led. Buchanan's article titled, "Global Warming: Hoax of the Century" consists of six bullet points and some commentary, altogether amounting to an impressive total of about two pages of text. Two of these points highlight what seem to be mere typos in the Intergovernmental Panel on Climate Change's 2007 report—one being an exaggerated percentage of Holland's sea level, and the other being a misreport concerning Himalayan glaciers (Buchanan 2). The other four points are similar attempts at global warming-contradicting facts, but without any references or cited support for his facts, Buchanan lacks the credibility or research depth to be noticed. Even if some of the points were true, such as his claim that the Antarctic sea ice cap is increasing in size, he lacks the scientific background to translate this occurrence into definite proof against the crisis of global warming (2). Perhaps the rate of Antarctica's growth has slowed but not reversed, or perhaps it would continue growing at a constant rate despite the warming of the biosphere. Buchanan simply states the phenomenon, which proves nothing. Such writing is comparable to an eavesdropping child asking his educated, environmentalist mother one night, "Global warming? But I feel cold!" The amount of research represented and cited by the fifty credible experts of DiCaprio's documentary is far too much to be affected by random opposing columnists who don't put references for their few bullet points of disproof.

From the many well-known, credible experts to the incorporation of emotion and logic, *The 11th Hour* constructs a strong argument concerning the seriousness of Earth's global warming crisis, and ultimately encouraging action. Admittedly, excess interviews can prove dry and tedious for an audience, but the purpose of the film was to be informative, not perfectly entertaining. The film's call to action—asking society to re-evaluate everything we do—seems at first to be an overwhelming task. As with all major difficulties, however, there is another way of looking at our circumstances in which we think like Paul Hawken of the film, "What a great time to be born, what a great time to be alive, because this generation gets to . . . completely change this world." So like the frog in the boiling pot, let us realize the danger we are in and leap out of it as individuals and a united world, into decisions and policies that are environmentally friendly, truly making us "green."

Caleb Knight is kinesiology major.

WORKS CITED

Bisland, Beverly Milner (Lee), and Iftikhar Ahmad. "Climate Change Draws World Attention: The Nobel Peace Prize Goes To Gore And IPCC." *Social Education* 72.2 (2008): 69-74. *Academic Search Elite*. Web. 30 Nov. 2011.

Bryan Walsh, et al. "Why Green is the New Red, White and Blue. (Cover Story)." *Time* 171.17 (2008): 45-57. *Academic Search Elite*. Web. 2 Dec. 2011.

Buchanan, Patrick J. "Global Warming: Hoax of the Century." *Human Events* 66.9 (2010): 15. *Academic Search Elite*. Web. 2 Dec. 2011.

The 11th Hour. Dir. Leila Conners Petersen and Nadia Conners. Prod. Leila Conners Petersen, Leonardo DiCaprio, Chuck Castleberry, and Brian Gerber. By Leila Conners Petersen, Nadia Conners, and Leonardo DiCaprio. Warner Independent Pictures, 2007.

CONSIDER THIS

- *At the beginning of his essay, Knight recounts a familiar anecdote. What is the relationship between this anecdote and Knight's analysis of* The 11th Hour?
- *Though you may not have seen the documentary* The 11th Hour, *are you still able to follow Knight's analysis? Does he provide enough context and summary to help guide readers who are unfamiliar with the argument made in DiCaprio's film?*

WRITER'S MEMO

I have been traveling by plane since before I could speak, so I have experienced the gradual increase in airport security. I remember the new screening methods that required shoes to be taken off and liquids to be confiscated, but now with the continued terrorist attacks resulting in the implementation of the full body scanners, I began to wonder just how successful these airport security measures really are. My research brought me to the realization that American airport security was in need of a change. The most difficult part of constructing this research paper, after obtaining my sources, was organizing the different propositions of reform into clear ideas that were easy for the reader to follow and understand. At the conclusion of this essay, however, I felt as though I had a strong case backed by evidence to support my claims.

Analyzing Methods of Improving Airport Security

Nicole Dennis

Every experienced flyer knows to arrive at the airport by 6 AM if they have an 8 AM flight. This two hour leeway may seem like an unnecessary buffer, but recently implemented government regulations for airport security have made check-in and screening lines a stress-filled nightmare for those who cut their arrival time too close to departure. Stewart Baker confronts airport security issues in the 2010 article, "Groping toward security: how to improve TSA screening," which was published in the *National Review*. Stewart effectively argues his position on the need to revise the current Transportation Security Administration (TSA) regulations through the use of logos and personal experience.

One of the main claims in Stewart's article is that in order to be taken seriously, opposers of TSA need to offer something better; they need to offer practical change, not just demand it. Stewart justifies this claim by appealing to the logic of readers and offering two solutions to the impending security problem. In the first solution, he rejects the idea of unionization when he writes that, "It [the patience and professionalism of TSA employees] required a commitment to disciplining and culling workers who aren't temperamentally suited to the job" (Baker). By drawing attention to the calm and professional attitude of the security personnel, readers realize that they are in fact uncannily patient with grumpy travelers, an uncommon trait in government workers. This was possible through the weeding out of workers who did not meet TSA criteria for behavior. The author then goes on to remind readers that culling is precisely what unions seek to stop, so if they would like to continue to be treated with dignity and respect by airport security, unionization must be prevented.

In the second solution he points out that, "The TSA's focus on finding weapons rather than terrorists is its biggest flaw" (Baker). Stewart breaches the sensitive subject of racial profiling by suggesting that the TSA needs to focus more on thorough searches of high risk individuals, rather than on broad and shallow searches of everybody. Readers will agree that grandma should not receive the same treatment as a young man returning from six months in Waziristan. On the surface, the difference between searching for terrorists and searching for weapons seems slight, but after applying critical thinking, drastic differences emerge. Stewart is implying that the productivity and efficiency of airport security will greatly increase by focusing the goal of the TSA to a more intelligence-based screening system, in which high risk individuals are flagged and scrutinized, while others get through with adequate, but less invasive, inspection. Not only does the author provide logical evidence and reason for his claim of the need to revise the TSA's regulations, but he also calls for revision through his personal experiences.

Stewart Baker adds to the article's effectiveness by using personal experience regarding the new TSA screening regulations, which he gained when he attended the National Opt-Out Day. Even though National Opt-Out Day ended up being a complete bust, Stewart, curious to see what all the fuss was about, still chose to opt-out. He describes his experience to readers by exclaiming, "That's it? I've had experiences that were about as intimate getting a pair of pants fitted" (Baker). We've all heard the horror stories of those awful full-body scanners that take naked pictures of passengers to be used at the discretion of the security guard on duty, and the alternative of opting-out, and having a middle aged man grope where he shouldn't be groping, has not been painted in the most appealing light either. Stewart's personal story about having gone through the enhanced pat-down and coming out unscathed, serves as an eye-opener to readers who have been plagued with false or exaggerated data.

LOOK HERE

The popular NPR show Democracy Now *broadcasted a segment on full-body scans that looks at the argument from a variety of viewpoints. You can watch the video here:*
http://www.democracynow.org/2010/11/19/national_outcry_over_tsa_body_scanners

Readers can take Stewart's personal experience as evidence that the media and human speculation has perhaps blown the scare-factor of these new security measures way out of proportion. Not only has Stewart had experience in dealing with security as a citizen, he has also had a personal hand in the governmental aspect. He demonstrates by saying, "When I worked at the Department of Homeland Security, we rewrote the TSA's rules and procedures more or less overnight when we discovered the liquids plot to blow up several transatlantic flights. We could not have done that if we'd had to bargain over the changes first" (Baker). This story reinforces Stewart's view that unionization of the TSA is a bad idea. This unique perspective, told by someone with a direct hand in the matter, is one that is not commonly seen by people, and it adds to the effectiveness of how he gets his point across to readers. When readers see the benefits of not being unionized, and how steps towards safety can be taken in a timelier and more efficient manner, they are more likely to be swayed to support Stewart's position to not unionize airport security.

Abolition of airport security is not what Stewart Baker is seeking to accomplish. He is quite in favor of having regular checks and screens of passengers; however, he does call for a revision of the current TSA regulations. He persuades readers to agree with his view point by making claims which appeal to their logic, such as stopping TSA unionization and redirecting the main goal of the program to finding terrorists, rather than merely weapons. He effectively brings in personal experiences, both of being a victim of search as well as being the implementer of regulation, to strengthen his argument. Stewart's clear and effective defense of his arguments for revision will leave even the most defiant of opposers fumbling for a rebuttal.

Nicole Dennis is an animal science major.

WORK CITED

Baker, Stewart. "Groping toward security: how to improve TSA screening." *National Review* 20 Dec. 2010: 22. *Gale Opposing Viewpoints In Context*. Web. 15 Feb. 2012.

CONSIDER THIS

- *What are your views on the increasingly invasive nature of increased airport security? Does Dennis's essay change the way you feel about passenger screenings?*
- *Another key issue in this essay is the argument against unionization for TSA employees. Does the evidence Dennis provides convince you that unionization would only contribute to lower standards of treatment for passengers? Why or why not?*
- *Does Dennis appear to fairly depict Stewart's viewpoint? What makes her rhetorical analysis effective?*

Too Powerful To Stay In Its Own Commercial

Thomas Flowers

Through advertising, countless companies reach out to customers in an attempt to grasp their attention and their checkbooks. When creating an advertisement, a company must take into consideration a wide array of details ranging from whom they are trying to attract to how they are going to reach them. The trend in commercials has shifted from the old school tactics of informational speeches and catchy jingles to a more modern approach of presenting just about anything outrageous in order to make the audience remember a brand. Old Spice, a well-known men's body care company, has recently introduced a series of commercials that stretch the limits of media standards.

Through the innovative use of irrelevant humor and extreme volume, Old Spice creates an enjoyable experience that reaches a broad range of audiences while leaving the viewers with an unforgettable memory of the brand. Oddly enough, the ad begins with another product's commercial. The commercial starts when a pleasant looking young woman enters a laundry room. She begins to explain to the audience the effectiveness of the outdoor freshness Bounce bar she uses. A few seconds into her pitch, a far off noise begins to crescendo into the commercial. It starts as the whisper of a scream, and a few seconds later, it is full-blown, in-your-face yelling that is impossible to ignore. As the random noise reaches the peak of its volume, suddenly Terry Crews, a humongous and muscular man, bursts through the wall of the laundry room riding a jet ski, revealing the origin of the unseen noise. The woman, as one would expect, acts very surprised to see an enormous man burst through the wall of her room. Before she can question what is going on, Terry Crews begins yelling once again, "Old Spice body spray makes you smell like power! It's so powerful it sells itself in other people's commercials!" (Body Spray, Old Spice). Following his outburst, Crews turns to the woman and kindly states, "You smell like outdoor freshness." The woman, who has seemingly forgiven the man for ruining her wall and interrupting her mid-sentence, thanks him and begins to reply, "You smell like power." (Body Spray, Old Spice). Before the compliment is even out of her mouth, Terry Crews rudely interrupts her once again and screams, "Yea I do!" (Body Spray, Old Spice). He then flexes his pecs in a manly fashion, emitting noises of power tools in unison, followed by a dramatic exit of taking flight and bursting through the ceiling. From that point, the advertisement shifts screens to an image of the various body sprays that Old Spice offers. Once more, Terry Crews flies by the screen bellowing the word "power."

LOOK HERE

To view the commercial Flowers is analyzing, go to:
http://www.youtube.com/watch?v=PvYP_d2S1Pg

The most obvious element of this commercial is humor, and more specifically, humor that appears completely unrelated to, and out of place in the main feature. Though there is nothing funny about deodorizing spray, the advertisement for it is hilarious. The inclusion of what might be considered misplaced humor has become a popular trend in advertising as of late. According to Kellaris and Cline of Wiley Interscience, "Each year, billions are spent on advertising in national media, with as much as 30% of that on the placement of humorous ads." This statistic raises the question: what makes humor such an effective medium?

The nature of humor is to make people feel good. Its use in promoting a product is a "promising way to influence [the consumer's] decision" (Kellaris and Cline). Humor has been found to "elicit positive feelings . . . inspire a positive attitude towards the ad, increase source liking, and heighten persuasion" (Kellaris and Cline). The power of humor to "heighten attention [and allow] people to process brand claims more actively" (Kellaris and Cline) is an invaluable asset. In a world polluted by the production of millions of commercials, a brand must fight for attention. Many large companies such as Doritos, Coca-Cola, and Old Spice have abandoned straightforward and informative tactics in favor of applying humor.

At the end of this thirty-second clip, the audience finds themselves hysterically laughing as well as wondering what just happened. The pitch that they observed had almost nothing to do with the actual product. Their main focus was on the joke of the situation, but because it was so funny and the product happened to be incorporated, they most definitely will remember Old Spice body spray the next time they go to the store. By instilling humor-induced confusion, coupled with a joyful laugh for the customer, Old Spice effectively sears their brand name into the brains of the masses.

Humor is the main focus of the commercial, but there are more components at work. Another noticeable piece of this advertisement is the use of unnecessarily loud volume. The feature begins with a calm environment, but it is quickly and abruptly ended with the extravagant entrance of Terry Crews, screaming at the top of his lungs. Once the serenity is broken, it never returns, as Crews continues his rampage of extreme volume for the duration. In a study executed by Hank Cetola and Kathleen Prinkley of Adrian College, it was found that, "the greater the intensity of such environmental stimuli, such as noise . . . the higher the resulting level of arousal." They also concluded that, "there is substantial evidence that a close relationship exists between shifts in arousal level and . . . the pleasure and the reward value people receive from increasing or decreasing arousal" (Cetola and Prinkley). When a consumer receives pleasure and reward value from a commercial, a positive image of the product is created in their mind. The positive image is maintained by the viewer and recalled at the next opportunity to purchase such products.

There is no doubt that it is a jarring experience when Terry Crews bursts onto the screen yelling. Whereas at first it may seem unnecessary or even unpleasant, the reality of the situation is that because this commercial is so disruptively loud, it effectively clings to the customer's thoughts and has the affect of creating memory. This being said, there are some cases in which certain audiences will be turned off by features of the advertisement, including but not limited to the noise. The humor, noise, and sex appeal in the message may be considered annoying or irrelevant to elderly people who are more interested in the facts. Another group that may be alienated are races other than black and white. The two people in the commercial are a white woman and a black man; people of different ethnicities may be offended because they were left out or because they have prejudice against those groups.

Creating a commercial is a precise and tactical maneuver. Undoubtedly, in the pursuit of pleasing one group, the producer will turn others away. The goal is to balance the aspects of your pitch in order to gain maximum acceptance for the broadest range of viewers. When a company achieves this objective, they are rewarded with more business and, in turn, increased revenue. The Old Spice body spray commercial is well balanced because it appeals to a variety of observers. For example, it makes an attempt to please both men and women. The incorporation of a large masculine man such as Terry Crews attracts both genders sexually or athletically. Additionally, by emphasizing that "Old Spice body spray smells like power," the company is essentially gambling on a basic psychological theory that, "men seek power," As for the members of the two sexes that do not identify with these notions, the universally accepted medium of humor is used to tie up the loose ends.

Old Spice professionally produces commercials tailor-made for certain audiences using specific techniques. The fact that no single commercial can touch everybody is taken into consideration. They solve this puzzle by producing many advertisements aimed at different audiences, such as the pirate and housewife themed version. By doing this, they not only increase product awareness by changing the message, but they also increase the amount and range of people that they are able to reach. In addition, this specific commercial incorporates all of the essential elements of rhetoric necessary to making a point. A big, strong man like Terry Crews is credible to all men because he is an athlete in superior shape. The notion of power is logical to all humans, as our basic instincts drive us to acquire it. Finally, the most heavily incorporated element of the commercial is emotion, addressed through the sidesplitting comedy that provides the listener with a source of amusement. The overall effect of this creative and innovative way to circulate product awareness is a happy consumer and a profitable company.

Advertising in today's world has become a complicated endeavor that needs to be effectively executed in order to reach consumers and compete against other brands. The goal of the Old Spice commercial is to entertain the customer and hopefully to be rewarded with purchases in return. In appealing to a large portion of the population with the modern tactics of irrelevant humor and noise, combined with the age-old tactics of sex and power appeal, Old Spice is able to define itself in an ocean of competition and set itself atop the charts of men's body care.

Thomas Flowers is an agricultural business major.

WORKS CITED

Cetola, Hank, and Kathleen Prinkey. "Introversion-Extraversion and Loud Commercials." *Psychology and Marketing-Adrian College* (1986): 123-31. *Communication and Mass Media Complete*. Web. 8 Mar. 2012.

Old Spice Body Spray / Old Spice. Advertisement. *Youtube.com*. OldSpice, 1 Feb. 2012. Web. 8 Mar. 2012.

"Sigmund Freud Quotes." *Sigmund Freud Quotes (Author of The Interpretation of Dreams)*. Goodreads. Web. 10 Mar. 2012.

Van Kuilenburg, Paul, Menno D.T. De Jong, and Thomas J.L. Van Rompay. "'That Was Funny, but What Was the Brand Again?': Humorous Television Commercials and Brand Linkage." *International Journal of Advertising* 30.5 (2011): 795-814. *Communication Mass Media Complete*. Web. 8 Mar. 2012.

CONSIDER THIS

- *Why do you buy certain products? Do you make purchasing decisions based on commercials that provide accurate information or advertisements that tickle your funny bone, like the one described in this essay? Are you most persuaded by commercials that rely on emotion (pathos) or logic (logos)?*
- *Does Flowers cover the most important elements of these Old Spice commercials in his analysis? By looking at the different parts of the commercials, does he help you gain a stronger understanding of how they seek to persuade consumers?*
- *Has entertainment become more important than truth in advertising (or in the media in general)? Is it even possible to remain unaffected by advertising today?*

Inheritance

Javal Patel

One fine morning, the people of a village in Gujarat, a state in India, were bound to be woken up to the unpleasant sound of ringing bells, which none of them ever wanted to face. It was the first day of the month, meaning food collection day. Every month, thirty percent of the total harvesting was taken away by the British. The British ruled India for more than 300 years. They imposed two major taxes on the people of India: a thirty percent tax on food grown by farmers and a salt tax on everyone in the country. It was hard for people to survive; the farmers couldn't dream about making money because all of their profit went to taxes. Sayajirao Gaekwad was the king of Gujarat in 1866; the whole country was ruled by the British, but some parts were ruled by kings assigned by the British. The king could do whatever he wanted as long as the province paid taxes to the British.

My great, great grandfather lived in Gujarat; he was an ordinary farmer who paid the taxes regularly. Even in the worst times of the season when the harvest was low, he kept up with the high taxes. This unusual regularity in paying the taxes caught the king's attention. To everyone's surprise, one day four of the king's men showed up with all their instruments to make a wooden swing, and of course they brought their artistic skill with them. People living around their house were shocked, confused, and startled to see these men in the neighborhood. It was considered a big honor to receive a gift from the king, and it was something rare to find in a small village.

LOOK HERE

Take a virtual tour of Gujarat, India: http://www.gujarattourism.com/

The wooden swing is made out of red sandalwood with a rot-proof paint on it, which has helped preserve the swing for over 100 years. It is four feet long and about three feet tall. It looks more like a royal bench with hand rests on each side. The swing has four legs which makes it usable as a couch. The swing a wooden backrest with a banyan tree carved on it. The banyan tree symbolizes the root of knowledge and is the national tree of India. There are four brass bars about ten feet long, which were used to hang the swing from the top of the ceiling inside the house. A few weeks after the swing was made, the king himself visited the village for the first time in his rule over Gujarat. He visited our tiny house and sat on the swing himself. The whole village came to look at this magnificent piece of architecture. My grandpa said, "It was unbelievable how honored I felt when your great great grandpa told me this story"

The swing was a great addition to the family, but the fight for independence against the British was still on. High taxes were an easy way for the British to extract every penny they could from the people; the whole nation pretty much worked for the British. Fed up with the high taxes, my great great grandpa decided to relocate in the nearby city where he could start his own business. Along with all his belongings, he made sure to take the swing with him. It took him two years just to get started on his business of cotton trading. The British had imposed heavy tax on all kinds of businesses. Compared to farming, he made more trading cotton, so he kept on doing this until 1947, when India achieved independence. After independence he kept on expanding his business as much as he could, until 1952 when he merged with three other partners to form a bigger company with five manufacturing units. All these years, the swing always stayed with my great great Grandpa, and it became an important part of the family.

"When I was little I used to play on the swing all the time," explained my Grandpa. He has many stories attached to the swing from his childhood. Once he fell down from the swing and injured his right knee, which left a small scar. This scar reminds him of the swing and all the good memories he had during his childhood. He liked the swing so much that after coming back from school, instead of sitting at his desk he preferred to sit on the swing and do his homework. "At times, I would fall asleep on the swing," said my Grandpa. The swing became an important part of his life and the bond that he created in the childhood is still fresh in his heart.

My Dad and Grandpa have done an excellent job of preserving this great artifact. "Every month I make sure the swing is clean and none of its parts are being damaged by rain or any termites attacking the wood" explained my Dad. Currently, it is still intact and can hold the same amount of weight it used to four score and thirteen years ago. It still holds the shine it used to when it was made originally. When I look at this swing, I can see the attachment I have with my family. I never got a chance to see my great great Grandpa, but this swing is a great symbol of all the changes my family went through. It holds a blood connection with my ancestors and the entire struggle India went through for independence. Sometimes when I am sitting on the swing, I can imagine how the king was sitting in the same spot as me decades ago; it creates this eternal happiness and the honor to be part of the swing's life is incredible. Of all the things that changed from 1866 until now, the swing has quietly played a major role in the background.

When I first saw the swing, I thought it had an unusual style to it, but I never had any clue of all the interesting stories I would find out about it. Now that I know about the history behind it, I feel lucky enough to have this opportunity to restore this great artifact in the future. Also, I can see how everything else in the history rotates around the swing, while the swing just stays in the same state it was more than 100 years ago. It has lasted through four generations; I look forward to keeping the tradition going and no matter where I go, I will take the swing with me.

Javal Patel is a materials engineering major.

WORK CITED

Patel, Vithal. Personal Interview. 9 February. 2012.

CONSIDER THIS

- *Patel begins his analysis by developing the background context that leads to the introduction of the swing. How does this information help the reader understand the artifact's significance?*
- *Patel describes the swing but does not provide an image. Would an image have been useful for you as a reader? What would it add to the essay? How would an image help develop your analysis?*
- *Analysis is frequently integrated with the Profile Sequence. How would an object analysis like this one help a writer begin to develop a profile essay?*

Public Rhetoric

What issues do you care about most?

The Grand Old Flag
Photograph by Jon Bartel

This photograph focuses on a young boy with his flag. While at first glance the image seems rather sentimental or "cute," it may actually make some interesting and important arguments about our culture. In a post 9/11 world, most of us have come to see America and American-ism much differently than our parents perhaps did. Arguably one of the most central images in our cultural experience is the flag as an iconic representation of both patriotism and a reminder of our previously safer, freer society. This image asks the audience to consider the role of patriotism in seemingly mundane moments of even the youngest citizens' lives. What other arguments might this photo make?

WRITER'S MEMO

I do not, nor do I claim, to know all the ins and outs of investment banking; after all, I'm merely a kid—a greenhorn, a novice—in this subject. However, because of my supposed naivety I am driven not to automatically accept everything that is given to me, whether that be by the media, my professors, or even my own parents! Over the past year, America has been saturated with stories about the Occupy Wall Street Movement and I, being the curious "child," wanted to know what all the fuss was about. However, I was extremely dismayed to find that not only my fellow peers, but even the vast majority of adults in my life, actually had very little knowledge about the heart of the issue. Instead both groups tended to reiterate the ignorant dribble of criticism relayed by the media or their parents who mindlessly watched said media. This blind acceptance of information and knowledge will be the true downfall of our society. Which finally brings me back to my essay: do not accept this paper as fact. It does delve into the history of banking and the problems surrounding it, but only touches the surface; above all, my essay is simply a piece of argumentative rhetoric. Take it, read it, contemplate it, then make your own judgment, hopefully with research of your own. If my essay has convinced you to do just that, it has served its purpose.

Regulation Impossible

Josh Silo

The Great Recession: the economic collapse that decimated our financial district, massacred employment levels, and sent the huge majority of American citizens into an unforeseeable future of never-ending, spiraling debt. Except, that might be a bit of a stretch;[1] our financial district—and by that I mean Wall Street[2]—seems to be doing quite fine, or at least fine enough to "[hand] out year-end bonuses in 2008 totaling $39 billion" (Frailey 6). Frailey goes on to say how that number was "more than three times the combined profit of [the investment banks]" (6). There is clearly an issue when the very industry that propelled the economic collapse isn't condemned, but instead is inexplicably rewarded. How are they paying bonuses when the stimulus plan was based on bailing them out? Why is this happening? Well quite simply it's due to the very people that are feeling the most ill effects from this recession: the silent, ignorant majority.[3] Despite the complete oversaturation and abuse of the word "recession," many Americans—particularly the nation's youth—are completely oblivious to what that word really means and what really caused it in the first place. Going beyond that, most people don't even seem to care! There is no excuse for this apathetic nature; whether it is ignorance or the cry of unadulterated capitalism. This is not an issue that deserves any less than a call to action! The issue of investment banking goes beyond the business sector; it impacts our nation's people as a whole. As a business student—no, even simply as young adolescent about to enter the global economy[4]—I think it is imperative that all Americans in the workforce, especially the ignorant, adolescent majority, fully understand the impact of investment banking and how desperately we need regulation to prevent another such disaster from ever occurring again.

---

[1]Metanoia
[2]Metanoia
[3]Hypophora
[4]Metanoia

In order to fully understand the gravity of the current situation, a basic knowledge of the history behind investment banking, regulation, and deregulation, is absolutely imperative. Meyer Eisenberg, who lectures at Columbia Law School, stated that "One of the early causes of today's problems was the deregulatory ripple that started in the Reagan administration" (Carter 35). The reason deregulation is, and should be, looked at so disparagingly is because regulation was originally enacted in response to a very similar financial crisis to the one we are experiencing today: the Great Depression.[5] When the actual causation of the Great Depression was scrutinized "[t]he subsequent congressional investigation documented abuses that, if known, might have foretold the collapse—in particular, risky investments in securities by banks" (Jost 62). As a result of both the fiscal calamity and the ensuing investigation, there was enormous support from the American public to help build new laws regulating banking and securities. Congress listened: "The Glass-Steagall Act, passed in 1933, separated commercial from investment banking . . . " and shortly after "Congress passed the Securities Act, which required disclosure of financial information by companies issuing stock or other securities. A year later, the Securities Exchange Act created the SEC, regulated securities trading and gave the SEC power to write anti-fraud rules" (Jost 62). In layman's terms, the Glass-Steagall Act was a sort of safety belt that prevented investment banks from tapping into clients' savings accounts, forcing the firms to risk more of their own capital instead, and thus make them more accountable for their risky financial ventures. To make it even simpler, the banks would not make any speculative business risks because they themselves would also have something to lose. The SEC was created as a regulatory agency to keep these investment banks in check and prevent them from engaging in any other illegal acts that also facilitated the Depression.

So if these precautionary measures were in place, why was there an economic collapse in today's day and age 70 years after the Great Depression? The simple answer is that these safeguards were no longer in place, and in the case of the SEC, have become wholly ineffective.[6] "The Gramm-Leach-Bliley Act of 1999 repealed the Glass-Steagall Act . . . [t]he new regulatory structure permitted commercial banks many of the same powers as brokerages and investment bankers" (Carter 35). By passing this act, Congress severed the safety belt put in place during the post-Depression era, and effectively monopolized the banking industry. With a monopoly, comes the risk of excess and abuse of power, and that's exactly what happened. Investment firms used this period of deregulation, along with the growing derivative market, to take advantage of investors and the housing bubble, all for the sake of extorting every last penny, despite the consequences. Even though being a business student entails maximizing the amount of profit one can make, it should not be at the expense of the rest of the nation, nor would I like to make that money through this sort of pseudo-legality.

LOOK HERE

For an animated explanation of some of the issues raised in this rhetoric paper, watch this clip promoting financial reform published by WhiteHouse.gov:
http://youtu.be/icfefQzRfL8

Critics may argue that what the investment banks did wasn't illegal; after all, the SEC—the regulatory agency responsible for preventing any injustices—did not intervene. However, the

---

[5]Exemplum
[6]Hypophora

SEC has been more than inadequate as of late. Most noticeably "... the commission had been lambasted for missing glaring evidence of Bernard L. Madoff's vast Ponzi scheme" (Morgenson). Sure Madoff has been prosecuted but "[a] report by the SEC's inspector general showed the agency failed to detect Madoff's crimes despite a succession of ever-more-detailed tips going as far back as 1992" (Jost 57). Additionally, according to a recent New York Times article entitled, "Is Insider Trading Part of the Fabric," the SEC knows that they have been less than satisfactory and have been attempting to hide their inadequacies through the false perception that they have been successfully convicting criminal acts in Wall Street, which they indeed have, but "... many involved minor players and small sums" (Morgenson). This is not to say that these cases aren't worth pursuing,[7] but it's quite suspicious when cases like the $50 billion Madoff-Ponzi case do not receive the same scrutiny, not to mention the overabundance of evidence! Not only has deregulation been sweeping the industry, but the little regulation that has remained has been clearly ineffective.

However, despite the evidence of correlation between current investment banking and the recession, there is still opposition to the reenactment of regulation. Some critics claim that by regulating the industry, we would infringe our nation's sacred tradition of capitalism and freedom. According to John Talbot, the mindset of the majority of the critics is that "[f]ree-market capitalism works best with no regulation and no interference from government" (29). John Talbot was a former investment banker for Goldman Sachs—one of the most prestigious firms on Wall Street—and thus would fit under the mold that regulation is an infringement. However, it's quite the opposite; he's vehemently against that perception. Talbot contends that "[t]rue students of economics will understand that there can be no free markets without regulation ... Laws, regulations, and rules are exactly what capitalism needs to survive" (29). Talbot does relent that there is such a thing as excess regulation, but he argues that's not America's problem right now for "[w]e have a free enterprise system that not only is unregulated, but one in which industry is writing its own regulations by controlling congressmen in Washington through campaign donations and lobbying" (29–30).[8] In other words, Talbot is implying there is a clear conflict of interest between the lawmakers and investment banks. Talbot evidences this claim by stating that "[h]edge funds on Wall Street are the largest contributors of Congress ... In 1999, banks paid Congress to repeal Glass-Steagall. In 2001, Congress was paid to not impose any regulations on derivatives. In 2004, commercial banks, another major contributor to Congress, were allowed to increase their financial leverage from ten times to over forty times their equity base" (30). Basically, banks were using their enormous wealth to change the law, all in order to decrease their accountability and thus increase their profits at the cheap expense[9] of the rest of our nation's financial stability.

If all this seems hopeless, that's because it almost is. Talbot says regulation is necessary for capitalism, but how can we create laws that regulate when our own Congressmen have their pocketbooks lined with investment firms' dirty money? The answer is simple: democracy.[10] We, the people, have the right to vote for our Congress and thus change the members who are participating in such despicable practices. I do relent, however, that even this is quite an impossible task[11] "[w]hile the regulations are initially passed by activists interested in limiting business power, over time the activists lose interest and the businesses themselves take over the

---

[7]Aporia
[8]Procatalepsis
[9]Understatment
[10]Hypophora
[11]Aporia

regulatory bodies and use them to minimize competition and maximize profits" (Talbot 230). He contends that we as citizens will lose interest as parties, but to that I say in this instance, we simply can't afford to lose interest. Even though I'm merely a first-year business student, the audacity of the investment banks has never made me care about anything more than this. Lose interest? Once such knowledge is known, interest will just grow stronger.

After the Great Depression, Americans were eager to impede, circumvent, and most of all, prevent[12] another catastrophe like that occurring ever again. Americans need that same fiery passion for change to bring to justice those who brought upon the financial hardships we all face today and those yet to come. Unfortunately, this will never be the case until America understands what really happened. Through knowledge, comes passion; through passion, comes change. At the end of the day, what the investment banks did can be summarized as such: "People break laws under the influence of greed—or they do only what's best for themselves, at the expense of everyone else" (Frailey 6).[13] What investment banks were doing was creating a win-win situation; when their clients won, they won big and when the clients lost, well, they lost almost nothing in return. That kind of system led to riskier and riskier investments until America couldn't handle the debts and the investment firms lined their pockets. Regulation is necessary. This is not something that can go on any further. This goes beyond business, beyond economics, beyond laws;[14] this is our future. This is something everyone needs to care about.

Josh Silo is a business administration major.

WORKS CITED

Carter, Terry. "How Lawyers Enabled: The Meltdown." *ABA Journal* 95.1 (2009): 34–39. *Academic Search Elite.* Web. 14 May 2012.

Frailey, Fred W. "My Take on Greed." *Kiplinger's Personal Finance* (Apr. 2008): 6. *Academic Search Elite.* Web. 14 May 2012.

Jost, Kenneth. "Financial Misconduct." *CQ Researcher* (Jan. 2012): 53–76. Web. 20 May 2012.

Morgenson, Gretchen. "Is Insider Trading Part of the Fabric." *The New York Times* (19 May 2012). Web. 20 May 2012.

Talbot, John. *The 86 Biggest Lies on Wall Street.* New York: Seven Stories Press, 2009. Print.

CONSIDER THIS

- *Silo uses footnotes to identify the rhetorical devices he relied on to bring greater complexity and depth to his writing style. Even if you are unfamiliar with the devices Silo uses, study the footnoted passages to further examine his stylistic choices.*
- *Follow this link to see definitions of these devices as well as additional examples illustrating how they are commonly used in speeches and other mediums to aid in the art of persuasion: http://www.americanrhetoric.com*
- *When first introduced to rhetorical devices, writers may feel a bit heavy-handed and awkward as they integrate these tactics into their prose. If rhetorical devices are new to you, select a paragraph you have recently composed and try to incorporate two or more of these rhetorical devices into your own work. How does this stylistic technique change or enhance your writing?*

[12]Scesis Onomation
[13]Setencia
[14]Asyndeton

WRITER'S MEMO

As a student who is pursuing a career in the education field—more specifically Special Education—I care about the "worthiness" of each student. Even if they have a mental or physical disability, I still believe they are able to contribute to our society; but, we need to give them that chance. Organ donation has always been a highly discussed topic, especially when it comes to receiving an organ. During my first year at Cal Poly, I came across an article about a little girl who needed a transplant. However, the doctors would not go through with the procedure because she had a mental disability (and for other reasons, too). After reading this article, I wanted to research more about organ donation and how children with a disability are sometimes overlooked because they don't meet the criteria. I hope this essay will spark interest among other readers as well.

"Worthiness" of an Individual

Kiersten Demmond

"Many people with disabilities are . . . denied evaluation and referral for transplantation at the primary care level"
—Laura K. Egendorf, Greenhaven Press, 2009

Before 1990, with the passage of the Americans with Disabilities Act [ADA], individuals with both mental and physical disabilities were discriminated from medical treatment—more specifically, from receiving transplants. Doctors evaluated the perception of worthiness for each patient and believed "a valuable organ for an unvalued life" (Egendorf 46) was a waste of an organ. Even with the passage of the ADA, mentally disabled patients still continued to face several hurdles. For instance, in 1995 Sandra Jensen, a 34-year-old Down Syndrome woman was in critical need of a heart and lung transplant. She was approved by her insurer, MediCal, and was then sent to two California transplant centers (Egendorf 46). Here is where the hurdles began. While one center denied her "without ever [meeting] or examin[ing] her" (Egendorf 47) the other hospital "determined that she would be unable to understand the procedures and to follow complex medical regimens" (47). After these assumptions were made about Sandra, publicity pressured medical doctors to reverse their decision. They were extremely upset and shocked about the doctor's decision. As a result, Sandra became the first mentally disabled patient to receive a transplant. There have been similar cases where people with mental disabilities have been denied transplants. Thus, there is a sense of inequity. Although this event happened 17 years ago, inequality between those who are disabled and those who are not is still an issue when it comes to organ donations. The hospital's reputation always seems to stand in the way of the patients' needs and they are not treated equally to those who are not mentally disabled.

While one is on the transplant waiting list, there is a long journey standing in front of them. As patients wait by their bedside, with their pager on the night stand, they hope that their time to receive a transplant is right around the corner. While some patients receive what they need, others are overlooked because they do not meet the criteria. "On average, 106 people are added to the nation's organ transplant waiting list each day—every 14 minutes" (Ethnics 14) according to the UNOS website. There is a lack of people willing to donate their organs which could accommodate the individuals in need of a transplant. Furthermore, about "17 patients die every day while awaiting an organ" (Ethnics 14) and are not given a chance at life. UNOS has set criteria in order to fairly allocate scarce organs; however, several groups are still discriminated from this set of criteria because they are seen to have an unvalued life. When do we draw the line between patients who have a mental disability and those that do not? How do doctors decide which recipients will receive an organ first? Do they require a different set of criteria for those that have a mental disability? All these questions stir up several other opposing viewpoints about how individuals can get on the waiting list—especially when scarcity of a valuable organ is involved.

Distribution of organs is based on a medical need basis, probability of success, and the amount of time the patient has been on the waiting list. Despite a patient's mental disability, there should be no excuse for an individual to receive a transplant unless there are other medical risks. As stated in the Hippocratic Oath—a covenant—doctors must "remain a member of society, with special obligations to all [their] fellow human beings, those sound of mind and body as well as the infirm" (1). Doctors should never make medical judgments on any patients no matter what the circumstances are. Even though adults with mental disabilities may not be able to give consent because they do not understand the conditions of receiving a transplant, this should not be a reason for a patient to not receive a transplant. Instead their family usually can understand the transplant procedure. Scarcity of organs may cause some doctors to make the argument about "the perception of worthiness" (Ethnics 14). Sandra's case exemplifies how individuals with mental disabilities "may be excluded from transplantation by transplant professionals" (Egendorf 48) because sometimes doctors "lack specific expertise in evaluating . . . the capabilities of disabled persons to comply with post-surgical regimens" (Egendorf 48). Furthermore, a convention was established by Don MacKay, in May 2004, because "650 million people in the world living with disabilities" (United 1) still faced several obstacles from obtaining proper health care. In Article 10 of the Convention of Rights for People with disabilities, state parties "reaffirm that every human being [should have] the inherent right to life" (United 1). All individuals, both disabled and non-disabled, should be treated equally unless there are critical reasons that a patient should be treated differently because of other health risks. Overall, someone not understanding a transplant procedure should not be the deciding factor on how worthy an individual is to receive a transplant. Instead, doctors should examine each patient individually, equally, and determine their decision based on the patient's medical needs.

Sometimes hospitals deny a mentally disabled person's request for a transplant because they do not believe they can reach their goal of maximum benefit—"maximizing the number of successful transplants" (Ethics of Organ Transplants 16). Timothy Shriver, chairman of Special Olympics, claims "people with intellectual disabilities who have been lucky enough to get a transplant do as well if not better than non-disabled people" (1). Therefore, medical doctors cannot assume that a mentally disabled patient will benefit less because of his or her condition. They must overlook all aspects of the patient's illness before coming to a final consensus—because we never know when one transplant can save an individual's life.

When doctors sit down and decide if a patient is going to receive a transplant they want to know how well he or she is going to respond to post-transplant care. After a transplant is given, recipients have to take several medications that will stop the rejection of the organ. Amelia may also encounter another threat: seizures. Carey explains, "anti-seizure medicine can speed up the metabolism, making it harder to calculate the right dose of immune-suppressing drugs that must be taken to prevent rejection of a transplanted organ" (1). Therefore, these issues may cause a bigger challenge, but should not be a concrete reason not to go through with a transplant if the parents believe the benefits will outweigh the costs. Amelia's doctor, from Children's Hospital of Philadelphia, mentions, they do not "disqualify potential transplant candidates on the basis of intellectual abilities" (James 3) as stated in an ABC news article; instead the medical team is "committed to providing the best possible medical care to all children" (James). In the end, the doctors care about the safety of each patient; however, there still seems to be a bias between the disabled and those that are not.

In January 2012, another story ignited "37,000 signatures on a petition . . . urging a hospital to change its initial decision" (Avril 1) on giving a mentally disabled patient a transplant. Three-year-old Amelia Rivera has Wolf-Hirschhorn syndrome which causes mental impairment, epileptic-like seizures, and kidney failures. She is in extreme need of a kidney transplant, otherwise she may die in the next six months to a year. As the family entered the doctor's office, they thought the decision to give their daughter a kidney transplant would be quite simple because of her medical need. To their surprise it was the exact opposite. Even twelve years after Sandra's case, mentally disabled patients still seem to be denied by medical professionals from receiving a transplant because doctors assume their condition cannot handle transplant procedures. According to Steven Reiss, people of all ages with mental disabilities do have success with receiving transplants after one to three years of receiving the transplant. The Organ Procurement and Transplantation Network, "reported national patient survival rates for renal transplantation of 95% at one-year follow up an 90% at three-year follow up" (Martens 8); therefore, the survival rates among those who are disabled are similar to the general population.

Throughout the decision in granting Amelia an organ, there were conflicts between primary care and the medical doctors. They seem to care more about their own reputation and the success of the procedure instead of the patient's medical need. A Philadelphia physician stated, "the hospital would not perform a transplant because of the girl's mental disability" (1). On the other hand, Pennsylvania hospital officials said they "[did] not make decisions on whether to do a transplant based on a patient's intellectual ability" (1); instead doctors wanted to test Amelia to see if she would be a good candidate based on other health concerns that are a result of her disability. Therefore, such conflicts affect the patient's hope in receiving a transplant because there is no clear consensus which will award a mentally disabled patient with an organ.

In Amelia's case, she was first denied the transplant because she was "mentally retarded" (Caplan), but after further investigation doctors soon discovered other severe issues which may harm her health. They knew the costs of the transplant will outweigh the benefits and even with a transplant her life may not be saved. Yet, according to the Americans with Disability Act (ADA), passed in 1990, discrimination against people with disabilities in medical treatment is prohibited. However, the Joint Commission on Accreditation of Healthcare Organizations claim, that people with disabilities still "face significant hurdles to being assessed for, wait-listed, and eventually receiving donor organs" (Egendorf 46). Doctors somehow find other reasons for why patients, such as Sandra and Amelia, can't receive a transplant. They base their decisions off how successful the transplant will be—how many years of life the recipient will have after given the transplant—and the patient's "inability to follow medical regiments" (Egendorf 47) after the surgery.

LOOK HERE

To further explore the complex issues surrounding Amelia's struggle, read Michele Goodwin's blog post in The Chronicle of Higher Education:
http://chronicle.com/blogs/brainstorm/too-disabled-for-an-organ-transplant/43265

Even though, I do agree that people who are extremely sick should receive an organ before others; I do not think the probability of success should be a criteria for a patient waiting for a transplant. Amelia is severely in need of a transplant or else she may die in the next 6 months; therefore, she meets the medical need requirement. On the other hand, medical success is difficult to predict and there is no define answer of what success is. Is success the number of years a patient lives after a transplant? Or is success the number of years a transplanted organ functions" (Ethics 17)? According to such questions, we truly don't know what a successful transplant is. Instead, doctors have biased outlooks on which patients can receive transplants and why others cannot. They did not want to grant Amelia a transplant because they knew her condition would cause other issues and there may not be a high success rate of the organ working. Geneticist John C. Carey, professor of pediatrics at the University of Utah School of Medicine, claims, "20 percent of people with [Amelia's] condition die in the first year or two, but once past that hurdle, they often live for decades" (Avril 1). As a result, there is still hope for those who have a mental disability if we give them a chance.

Although, this topic raises several other ethical issues, it is impossible to cover and relate them all at once. The main issue here is that individuals with a mental disability should be treated no differently than those that have no disorder. Everyone is worthy of a transplant and the medical need should be the main reason doctors use to allocate organs. Regardless of the mental disability, I hope medical fields acknowledge the worthiness of all patients and grant opportunities that may save a life.

Kiersten Demmond is a liberal studies major.

WORKS CITED

Amelia Rivera. www.abcnews.go.com. 23 Feb. 2012. Photograph.

Avirl, Tom. "Children's Hospital Reverses Decisions not to Perform Disabled Girl's Transplant." Opposing Viewpoints. *Philadelphia Inquirer*. 31 Han. 2012. 14 Feb. 2012.

Caplan, Art. "Serious Issues in Disabled Girl Transplant Case." Vitals. N.p. 17 Jan. 2012. 23 Feb. 2012.

Egendorf, Laura K. "The Organ Transplant Process Is Biased Against the Disabled." Organ Donation: Opposing viewpoints. Maine: Greenhaven Press. 2009. 45–49. Print.

"Ethnics of Organ Transplantation." Center for Bioethics: University of Minnesota. Feb. 2004. 7 Feb. 2012.

Equal Access for All. www.fairuselab.net. 24 Feb. 2012.

Hippocratic Oath Definition. www.medterms.com. 1 March 2012.

James, Susan Donaldson. "Amelia, Mentally Disabled, May Get Kidney Transplant After All." *ABC News*. N.p. 31 Jan. 2012. 2 Feb. 2012.

Little Boy with Down Syndrome. www.mychildwithoutlimits.org 10 March 2012.

Little Girl at Special Olympics. www.sodahead.com. 10 March 2012.

Martens, M. A., Jones, L. and Reiss, S. Organ Transplantation, Organ Donation and Mental Retardation. Pediatric Transplantation, 10: 658–664.

Shriver, Timothy. "No Room at the Inn." *Washington Post*. N.p. 25 Dec. 2006. 16 Feb. 2012. Print.

CONSIDER THIS

- *Any effective argument must strike a balance between* ethos, pathos, *and* logos. *Did Demmond effectively develop her credibility? Was her logic sound? And did she help you develop an emotional investment in this issue—a subject you may have never thought about before?*
- *As Demmond's essay demonstrates, there is seldom just two viewpoints to consider when developing an argument. Can you identify the many different viewpoints she works to account for in this essay?*

The fastest, simplest way to stay close to everything you care about.

Joey Catanzarite

So reads the masthead of the "About" section on Twitter. Having used Twitter myself for over a year now, I would tend to agree that this is the easiest way to describe to an uninformed person what exactly Twitter is. Twitter is a social media site that allows the user to inform the world what is on their mind. Since its creation in 2006, Twitter has allowed the user to do just what the websites description says: stay close to everything you care about. This could be family, friends, sports teams, or celebrities. However, since the 2008 presidential election, many politicians have begun to use Twitter as a tool: a tool to stay close to *you*. In this day and age, politicians are encouraging young people to become the driving force behind political issues. Politicians are now turning to social media, such as Twitter, to reach out to the youth of America in an attempt to harness their youthful passion to shape the political issues of this day.

Barack Obama's election in 2008 marked a significant event in American history: It was the first time an African-American was elected to the office of president. However, this election also marked another important, yet less talked about, historical mark. According to Damien Cave, writer for *The New York Times*, Obama's victory in the 2008 election was largely due to his younger supporters. More 18 to 29 year olds voted in this election than in any election since 1972. Around 23 million eighteen to twenty-nine year olds voted, which is more than the 19.4 million that voted in the 2004 election. It is estimated that around 66 percent of these 18 to 29 year olds voted for Obama. Now how was it that Barack Obama was able to inspire so many young people to come out and vote? Cave believes that he was largely able to do this through informal communication to the people via Twitter, Facebook, and emails. All of these were aimed to communicate directly with the people in order to make them feel involved in the campaign. Obama's direct, yet informal communication style proved to make him a much more relatable figure (Cave). Twitter is providing politicians with the ability to mobilize young voters with great success. If the trends from the 2008 election continue, then Generation Y, which has typically been stereotyped as not caring about politics, may continue to become much more politically involved.

Generation Y has grown up in an era unlike any other. Never before has a wide range of information been instantly available with a few clicks of a button. However, as Generation Y has matured, so has the Internet itself. Research specialist Aaron Smith found that the overall size of the political news audience online has more than doubled since the 2000 elections. This audience searching for news online is composed of mostly young people. According to Smith, "30% of those who post political content online are under the age of 25, and more than half are younger than 35. Political content creation is also tightly linked with the use of social media platforms such as online social networks, video sharing sites, blogs and status update services such as Twitter." With knowledge that the youngest voting generation was largely in support of him, Obama therefore used the platform that would best reach his audience: the Internet. As a result, Obama voters were much more likely to be politically involved online than McCain voters. MSNBC writer Elizabeth Chuck noted that both presidential candidates used Twitter. However, Obama had over 112,000 followers while McCain had around 4,600 followers. This meant that Obama was able to directly communicate to twenty-four times as many people as McCain via Twitter. As a result, Twitter played an essential role in Obama's ability to capture the vote of the younger audience. His ability to do so led Obama to victory in an election that was all about change in America, as young Americans stood up to make this change reality.

Following the 2008 election, many political figures have joined the ranks of those on Twitter. There are currently over 100 million active users of Twitter, which is more than ten times as many users as there were during the 2008 election (Parker). As a result, Twitter has emerged as an increasingly important tool for politicians to reach out to voters, both old and young. Ashley Parker, writer for *The New York Times*, wrote, "If the 2008 presidential race embraced a 24/7 news cycle, four years later politicos are finding themselves in the middle of an election most starkly defined by Twitter, complete with 24-second news cycles and pithy bursts." Twitter allows one to be instantly connected to the world and provides the platform for constant political discussion. Politicians are reaching out to voters, while at the same time receiving instant feedback. Twitter allows politicians to gather data and target demographics specifically (Parker). For example, *The New York Times* writer Ashley Parker wrote, "Mr. Romney's aides say they can get a sense of where a story is headed before it is published simply by reading reporters' Twitter messages. If reporters have flagged a particular incident on Twitter—for instance, the woman who stood up at South Carolina event and asked Mr. Romney, a Mormon, if he believed "in the divine saving grace of Jesus Christ"—Mr. Romney's aides might pull him aside before a press conference and warn him that the topic is likely to come up." Twitter can therefore provide politicians critical information to aid the analysis of their desired audience. As a result, in the most recent presidential campaigns, both President Obama and his Republican opponents are using Twitter as a way to get their messages to the youth of America.

LOOK HERE

Want to know more about the ways in which both political parties are using Twitter? Visit the Huffington Post *at*

http://www.huffingtonpost.com/2012/05/07/twitter-2012-campaign-outsize-role_n_1494797.html

With all this use of technology, it seems that the stage is set for young Americans to again be the deciding factor in the 2012 presidential election. A *U.S. News* article recently released stated, "To win re-election, the president needs the same kind of enthusiasm and support from young people he enjoyed in 2008. The president will have to work very hard to capture the magic of his last campaign" (Bannon). Following an average first term, President Obama looks to rally passionate young supporters behind him again. In this election, Twitter is playing an even more crucial role to reach such demographics than the 2008 election. The median age of Twitter users is 31, compared to other social networking sites like Facebook (33) or LinkedIn, whose median age is 39 (Fox et al). This puts the age group on Twitter in an important demographic area that Obama is appealing to. Since the 2008 election, Twitter itself has evolved in ways that will help the candidate's messages be heard. You no longer need to follow a presidential candidate on Twitter to see what they are saying. According to *The New York Times* writer Ashley Parker, campaigns can now pay for promoted messages that will appear on the users home screen where all tweets appear, or be the top result when certain key words are searched. This means that these promoted messages will spread to more people than ever before. Given these facts, there's a chance that we could see a rise in the number of young voters at the polls again this year.

Every morning when my alarm clock rouses me from my sleep, the very first thing I do is roll over and pick up my phone. Before I check my texts or my emails, I open up the Twitter application on my Blackberry. I scroll past the tweets posted by my friends, stopping occasionally at the little picture icon of Barack Obama. Reading the presidents tweets every morning has become a ritual to me, something that I do before even leaving my bed. Before the 2008 election, I had no interest whatsoever in politics. After signing up for Twitter and following President Obama, my interest in politics has risen exponentially. Now that I am of age, I have every intention of voting in the 2012 presidential election. I can safely say that without Twitter, I would most likely enter the booth as an uneducated voter. Twitter has been a key tool in allowing me to quickly access political information and it has inspired my interest in politics. I am a part of Generation Y, and I know that I am not alone in my morning routine. For the casual follower of politics such as myself, Twitter has become the fastest, simplest way to stay close to everything I care about. When the time comes at last to cast my vote this fall, I will be one more member of Generation Y to make my vote heard. Without Twitter, who knows where I might otherwise be on November 6.

Joey Catanzarite is an agricultural business major.

WORKS CITED

Bannon, Brad. "Romney is Winning Young Voters . . . For Obama." *U.S. News*. U.S. News and World Report, 2012. Web. 5 May 2012.

Cave, Damien. "Generation O Gets Its Hopes Up." *The New York Times*. The New York Times, 2008. Web. 3 May 2012.

Chuck, Elizabeth. "140: The 2008 Election's Other Magic Number." Decision '08 Archive. *MSNBC*, 2008. Web. 3 May 2012.

Fox, Susannah, Kathryn Zickuhr, Aaron Smith. "Twitter and Status Updating, Fall 2009." Pew Internet & American Life Project. Pew Research Center Publications, 2009. Web. 5 May 2012.

Parker, Ashley. "In Nonstop Whirlwind of Campaigns, Twitter is a Critical Tool." *The New York Times*. The New York Times, 2012. Web. 3 May 2012

Smith, Aaron. "The Internet's Role in Campaign 2008." Pew Internet & American Life Project. Pew Research Center Publications, 2009. Web. 2 May 2012.

CONSIDER THIS

- *How have your political views been affected by your interactions on social media sites such as Twitter or Facebook? Are you likely to vote based on information gathered through this medium?*
- *How are the three appeals used in the context of social media-based rhetoric? Which of the three are most heavily relied upon by politicians seeking your attention and vote?*
- *As you read, consider the motives of elected officials who post on Twitter. Are their tweets meant to be informative, persuasive, or even entertaining? Can social media affect the outcome of an election?*

Deprived of the Means

Dayna Scott

"Some people call undocumented workers *illegals*, turning an adjective into a noun. In human history, when we turn an adjective into a noun to describe people, it's usually a way of dehumanizing them, of saying they're not really people by taking the people word out of it" (Daniel 29). People labeled by words so commonly spoken with hatred and revulsion are people just like us: people with hopes of successfully raising a family, people who dream of living in a welcoming community, and people who hope one day their children can do better things than they ever dreamed of. These citizen-seekers come here with the idea that it is the place where they can realize their hopes and dreams. Not only are these people willing to work hard at low paying jobs Americans stick their noses up to, but they are, above all, human. Just like anyone else with citizenship in the US, they are human.

Families come from all over the world seeking a place in the United States to fulfill their way of life better than where they came from. Naturally, when they come here, they bring their children along with them. Their children grow up learning the English language and going to school like many other children. When, or if, they finish their extent of public school, they are faced with the challenges that have been awaiting them since their arrival: how will they get a job? How will they get into college? How will they pay for college? How will they get citizenship? Many parents neglect to find answers to these important questions before coming to America and find themselves in a bind when forced to come up with solutions. The few choices immigrant children growing up in America have, consist of getting deported back to where they were born (where they are just as much a foreigner because they have no recollection of living there), or working somewhere that pays under the table for difficult manual labor in hopes of being able to afford citizenship at some point in their life. Most children who come from an illegal family do not consider college as an option, either because no one in their family had been before them, or the financial burden is too great: "While 95 percent of Latino parents want their children to attend college, 77 percent say this is impossible given the cost, according to the Pew Hispanic Center" (Horwedel and Asquith 25). Even for US natives, college is an expensive and challenging process, but the government offers little to no help to those who are not natives.

LOOK HERE

To understand the fuller context surrounding terms like "illegal alien," read this article featured Forbes.com:
http://www.forbes.com/sites/timothylee/2011/09/30/society-of-professional-journalists-reporters-shouldnt-use-pejorative-terms-like-illegal-immigrant/

Recently, the government has made an attempt to reach out to immigrant students who are striving to become constructive citizens. Through the California Development, Relief and Education for Alien Minors (DREAM Act), children brought illegally in the US by their parents, or for other reasons, are given a glimmer of hope. Although this may seem like a helping-hand-gesture, the specifics of the DREAM Act, summarized by the *Congressional Digest*, significantly narrow the amount of people who qualify:

To be eligible, students would have to prove that they had been in the United States continuously for at least five years, were not yet 16 when they got here, were of good moral character, and had been admitted to an institution of higher education or had earned a high school diploma or the equivalent. This would give the students conditional permanent resident status. To achieve full LPR status, they would need to complete at least two years of college or serve for two years in the U.S. military. (Legislative 267)

Through this interpreted description of the DREAM Act, it almost seems easy to become a citizen while becoming an educated professional. However, when looking at the official proposal of the bill by congress, if you make it past all of the confusing legal terminology, you will find pages upon pages of technicalities involving loopholes that allow The Secretary of Homeland Security to cancel the conditional citizenship for numerous reasons. It's almost as if you sneeze at the wrong moment you are deemed ineligible and your conditional citizenship is revoked. The DREAM Act is most definitely a step in the right direction, but it still has some kinks it needs to smooth out.

The original bill set forth by Congress states as a requirement that the person applying for the DREAM Act must be "a person of good moral character since the time of application" (Appendix 90). However, it does not clearly state what 'good moral character' is, in fact. This is basically leaving the power open ended for the government to decide who is and who is not 'eligible' based on their interpretation of moral character. In some cases, it is fairly obvious that someone with a lengthy criminal record is indeed not someone of good moral character, but there are many other things that require further analysis.

Also, the DREAM Act can only help in the financial department on a state level. Under this Act illegal children are able to receive student loans and work study programs but not federal financial aid. Loans and work study programs are helpful, but most of these children come from low income families suffering from poverty. When it comes to the choice between racking up thousands of dollars in student loans, or getting a job to contribute to the family income, it seems apparent as to which they would pick. When Horwedel and Asquith surveyed common reasons as to why Hispanics would not enter or finish college; 77% agreed that the cost of tuition was an insurmountable feat. Equally high percentages suggested they needed to work to earn money, they did not receive a sufficient high school education, or they felt discrimination would deter their chances of acceptance (23). This only furthers the idea that money is the main hindrance keeping natural born Hispanics from conquering college. With all these reasons to hold them back, they must prove to those who object to the DREAM Act that they are worth the time, money and effort.

Many natives see the DREAM Act as an unfair way to use taxpayer's money. Republicans, who are generally the group most opposed to this measure, believe that passing this act would only "reward violators of the country's immigration laws and encourage new waves of illegal immigration" (Bradley 6–7). Bradley also records the Republican view that it only requires two years of higher education or military service, which in their opinion, is too low of a standard.

Americans tend to think strictly in terms of the now, the present. Sometimes looking into the future may be beneficiary. Education Secretary Arne Duncan states her fears of the US not meeting their quotas; "The US will be short 3 million college graduates from what the market will demand in 2018 in the fields of science, technology, engineering, and mathematics" (qtd. in Hudson 18). Passing this act with benefit the country in a way that will increase the number of college graduates in the fields that are predicted to be lacking; therefore, the money spent to financially help immigrants receive a higher education will not be wasted, but will contribute to the country to continue being competitive among other countries of the world.

Moreover, children brought here by their parents are typically very young and have no conscience of the laws they are breaking by coming to the US. By the time they are old enough to understand the laws, they have already considered the United States their home for years, and have no other options since typically their entire family is in the country illegally. The standards set by the Act may be unsatisfactory to those opposing it, but it does not necessarily mean that people are only going to complete the bear minimum and drop out as soon as they gain citizenship, in most cases they want to get a better education to become successful and be able to provide for themselves and their families. Otherwise, if an immigrant is able to receive a degree, but is not granted citizenship, their talents are wasted seeing as they are legally unable to work in the US and contribute to their area of specialty. This seems like more of a waste of money than sending illegal children to school, who in turn, become citizens that constructively contribute to our society.

Overall the DREAM Act would benefit our society as well as those struggling to become citizens. Although it may have flaws, there is time to fix them before the measure is passed. As for any measure, there are always people who oppose it, or disagree with what it stands for. In this situation, it seems that the positive aspects outweigh the negative. Everyone deserves a chance, and this chance is given by guiding them in the direction to become a constructive citizen. Natives of our country are granted citizenship at birth, while these children brought here without choice have to jump through hoops in hopes of gaining the perks associated with citizenship. All they are trying to do it create a better life for their future generations by doing what their parents could never do for them.

Dayna Scott is a civil engineering major.

WORKS CITED

"Appendix: The Dream Act Of 2009." *New Directions For Student Services* 131 (2010): 85–93. *Academic Search Elite*. Web. 2 Nov. 2011.

Bradley, Paul. "Outlook 2011. (Cover Story)." *Community College Week* 23.11 (2011): 6–7. *Academic Search Elite*. Web. 9 Nov. 2011.

Daniel, Lillian. "Immigrants Like Us." *Christian Century* 127.19 (2010): 28–33. *Academic Search Elite*. Web. 2 Nov. 2011.

Horwedel, Dina M., and Christina Asquith. "For Illegal College Students, An Uncertain Future." *Diverse: Issues In Higher Education* 23.6 (2006): 22–26. *Academic Search Elite*. Web. 8 Nov. 2011.

Hudson, Audry. "DREAM Act Dreamers: Wake Up!." *Human Events* 67.24 (2011): 18. *Academic Search Elite*. Web. 9 Nov. 2011.

"Legislative Background On The DREAM Act." *Congressional Digest* 89.9 (2010): 267. *Academic Search Elite*. Web. 8 Nov. 2011.

CONSIDER THIS

- *Scott starts her essay with a quotation before she provides readers with any context for her argument. Is this an effective way to introduce her claim/thesis? Would the quotation be more effective if it were used later in the introduction?*
- *Examine how Scott addresses opposing viewpoints. Does she give enough consideration to her opposition? How could she develop this area?*
- *Scott's argument relies on strong* pathos. *What does* pathos *add to her argument? Does she balance* pathos *with logos? How does this rhetorical choice affect her overall argument?*

The End to Plastic Water Bottles

Megan Jones

The act of recycling has become an issue spread all around the world. Whether it is plastic bags or glass bottles, there are still inconclusive answers. The most recent concern is about the plastic bags in our landfills and oceans, killing animals around the world, and therefore hurting us in the end. However, it is important to also take plastic water bottles into consideration. Not only are they polluting our environment, the water in them is actually bad for our health as well. This is not only due to the greed of large water bottle companies, but also the selfishness and lack of knowledge most Americans possess.

In terms of pollution, plastic water bottles are contaminating pure water rivers around the world. The movie, *Tapped*, is an anti-plastic water bottle documentary describing all of the negative side effects of water bottles on our environment and us. "[In the] last couple years, the trash they are finding in rivers is plastic bottles, hundreds and hundreds of plastic drinking water bottles" (*Tapped*). Water bottle companies are making a profit while the pure water industries are suffering. This is not fair to pure water industries. Water bottles have become so convenient because, according to the documentary, *Tapped*, "We want everything individualized, personalized and just for us. We want to not have to wash it or take care of it. We want to be able to just throw it away, and we want it immediately available and convenient." This convenience, however, is only part of Americans' laziness.

LOOK HERE

See segments of the documentary Tapped *on YouTube:*
http://www.youtube.com/watch?v=72MCumz5lq4

Though recycling seems like an easy and feasible solution to this water bottle problem, Americans are too lazy to even do that much. According to *National Geographic Magazine*, "Only 13 percent of 29 billion bottles actually end up in a recycling stream" (Didier). Recycling does not completely fix the issue and yet Americans still do not put in effort to do that much. Even if everyone began recycling everything, it would not completely fix the pollution issue. Americans do not dispose of their waste properly, whether it is recycling or littering. "Up to 63.4 billion plastic bottles are dumped into landfills and the ocean a year. This is 173,589,044 a day, 120,548 every minute," stated by Jeff Bennett. This is an incredible number, just due to the plastic bottles. These statistics do not even include plastic bags or any other kind of plastic trash. Even if we were to clean up our waste and dispose of it correctly, it might not help solve our problem. According to Doug Gunzelmann in the *Green Updater* article, "plastic water bottles take 700 years to begin composting." Though recycling and/or throwing away our trash is a solution, I do not think it is the best one for our environment. The quickest and easiest solution to this pollution is to minimize the amount of plastic water bottles, not keep using them, and recycling. However, an average American is not the only one that can help clean this dilemma.

Recent studies show that bottled water companies are taking advantage of pure water industries. In most cases, they are actually taking tap water and selling it back to us for profit. From a buyer's standpoint, why would we purchase it when we could get it from the same source for free? In fact, "40% of bottled water is just filtered tap water" (*Tapped*). This being said, do you want to pay extra for something that you could get free? This seems like an inarguable no, yet Americans today still buy bottled water. It is ridiculous that companies today, such as Pepsi's Aquafina and Coke's Dasani, are making profit on something that we can get almost for free.

Not only are the large-scale companies taking advantage of Americans and pure water resources, Americans are not informed of the health benefits of tap water. Tap water is better than bottled water in that it contains fluoride. Fluoride is a mineral that helps prevent cavities in the mouths of all Americans today. According to the Kids Health Organization, "fluoride exists naturally in water sources . . . [and] helps prevent and even reverse the early stages of tooth decay." Bottled water does not contain this fluoride component because it is filtered out. In order to get this fluoride, it is simple enough to just drink tap water. In fact, "As of 2002, CDC statistics show that almost 60% of the U.S. population receives fluoridated water through the taps in their homes" (Fluoride and Water). This being known, why would we want to pay for bottled water as well as a dentist when we could just drink tap water and save the money for both.

Advocates of water bottles may push the idea that water bottles are convenient and can even be refilled to cut the amount of pollution down. As a track runner, I would often put two plastic water bottles in my backpack before practice. Because I had practice every day and did not want to be using that many water bottles. Instead, I reused these plastic water bottles for a couple days before recycling. Little did I know, the bacteria and heated plastic were contaminating my body. *Time Magazine* reports, "Many water bottles on the market are made of a hard plastic called polyethylene terephthalate, or PET. While the material is perfectly safe for single use, it's not designed for repeated reuse" (Cullen). This is because not only will bacteria build up around the bottle's mouth, the plastic is released into the water under warmer temperatures. Consequently, this requires Americans to buy more water bottles therefore resulting in more pollution. It is a never-ending cycle. The best solution is to reduce the amount of one-time use plastic water bottles.

Sure, it is convenient to have bottled water to grab for the go, but is it worth contaminating the environment and our bodies for that satisfaction? In order to reduce the amount of plastic water bottles today, many companies like Camelback are creating reusable water bottles. Even our Cal Poly Bookstore sells Camelback reusable water bottles. These bottles are perfect for filling up before a day out and about. Because they are reusable, they are not contaminating our environment. Also, because most people fill up their reusable water bottles with tap water, they are actually better for our health. Why not spend the money one time for a reusable water bottle as opposed to constantly buying one-time use plastic water bottles. Making this small change will help all of us live happier and healthier lives.

Megan Jones is an architecture major.

Works Cited

Bennett, Jeff. "Plastic Bottles & Ocean Pollution." *Plastic Bottles & Ocean Pollution*. 07 May 2009. Web. 01 June 2012. <http://www.slideshare.net/JeffBennett/plastic-bottlesocean-pollution-draft-1401540>.

Cullen, Lisa T. "Freshen Up Your Drink." *Time Magazine* 13 Mar. 2008. Web. <http://www.time.com/time/magazine/article/0,9171,1722266,00.html>.

Didier, Suzanna. "Water Bottle Pollution Facts." *Green Living on National Geographic. National Geographic.* Web. 01 June 2012. <http://greenliving.nationalgeographic.com/water-bottle-pollution-2947.html>.

"Fluoride and Water." *KidsHealth.* Ed. Steven Dowshen. Nemours Foundation, Apr. 2011. Web. 21 May 2012. <http://kidshealth.org/parent/growth/feeding/fluoride_water.html>.

Gunzelmann, Doug. "Plastic Bottle Facts Make You Think Before You Drink GreenUPGRADER." *Green Updater.* 23 Aug. 2008. Web. 01 June 2012. <http://greenupgrader.com/3258/plastic-bottle-facts-make-you-think-before-you-drink/>.

Tapped. Prod. Michael Walrath and Michelle Walrath. Atlas Films, 2009. Documentary.

CONSIDER THIS

- *Jones's essay makes strong claims about the habits of Americans. How do these claims help develop her pathos? Would certain audiences be offended or isolated by these claims?*
- *Jones offers a solution to the problem presented in her essay: she suggests people buy reusable water bottles. Is this solution feasible? What are alternative solutions to this issue?*
- *Jones uses the documentary* Tapped *as one of her sources. How does this choice help develop her ethos and logos?*

WRITER'S MEMO

When I tell people my major is in manufacturing engineering, they often ask about what I do since it is an uncommon field of study. My inability to provide a satisfactory answer prompted me to pick American manufacturing as a research topic for my essay. Not only is it relevant to my studies and future career, but I also quickly realized that it is a huge component of the struggle our country faces right now. In fact, after doing my initial research, I found I had far too much information to work with because everything connected. Structuring my essay to smoothly transition between and tie together each topic was one of my biggest challenges, as well as making sure my own voice was heard and not just my quotes. Still, I recommend picking a topic that truly interests you and to do the research. Editing out information because you have too much is always more desirable than scraping together bits and pieces.

Manufacturing America

Roxanne Raye

You've seen it in the news and heard it on the radio: America is losing jobs in manufacturing to foreign countries such as China and India. Fear quickly grips us at the idea of more jobs being lost in an already stumbling economy, and the thought of America no longer being on top stabs at our pride. But is that really the case, or just hyped up claims by the media? However, the better question may be what *is* manufacturing? Most will imagine a factory with an assembly where each worker does the same task repetitively all day, but there is more to it than that. My father, Steve Raye, a manufacturing engineer who has been working in the industry for 26 years, offers his explanation: "Manufacturing is not only figuring out how to actually make a part, but how to make it repeatedly without error." Despite what the media may say, the United States is still the leader in manufacturing high quality products. If we want to stay on top, however, there needs to be an increase in education geared towards math, science and engineering. From job creation and the economy, to education and international politics, manufacturing is more than just science.

It is no secret that in 2008 the United States entered a recession that skyrocketed unemployment. As of July 2011 the U.S. Bureau of Labor Statistics states in *CQ Researcher's* article "Reviving Manufacturing" that the United States has "a national joblessness rate of 9.2 percent [. . .]14.1 million people—out of 153.4 million working-age adults—are jobless, and another 8.6 million can find only part-time work" (Katel 603). Such a high percentage doesn't make sense when companies such as Siemens Corp., the U.S. arm of Germany's Siemens AG, report having "over 3,000 jobs open all over the country. [. . . and other] companies report job vacancies that range from six to 200, with some positions open for at least nine months" (Mutikani). The key problem is the people looking for jobs are not qualified for the ones that are open. For both large and small manufacturing companies, employers are looking for workers skilled in math, science and engineering, or with technical trade skills such as welding or mechanics. Tom Price, a Washington-based freelance journalist, discusses in *CQ Researcher's* article "Science in America" how "employers [. . .] say they have to hire foreigners because there aren't enough qualified Americans to do the jobs" (Price 29). As unemployment rates refuse to yield and more and more companies turn to outsourcing, the future looks bleak. There is still good news however, the "United States remains the world's high-tech leader by most measures. [...] America turns out more than a quarter of the world's economic product with less than a 20th of the world's population" (Price 28). The problem is not that America is drastically falling behind, but that the world is catching up and accelerating at a faster rate. That's where manufacturing engineers come in.

Look Here

In The Case to Strengthen US Manufacturing, *the filmmakers argue for the importance of American factories:*
http://www.youtube.com/watch?v=Si2-gotn5uE&feature=youtube_gdata_player

The United States has turned its eye on lean manufacturing, a process that cuts down on human error in factories often by implementing robots. The idea is to be better with less. Raye, my father, is currently working with a team of engineers at Blount International, a chainsaw company, to redesign their product flow. When asked how he felt about his project's success eventually causing other people to lose their jobs, he replied, "I hate to think I'm taking away jobs from people, but making things more efficient is how we stay competitive." Competition is everything in business and price is a huge sticking point. The less a company has to pay workers the cheaper they can sell their product. Once a robot is installed it can work long hours, but not everyone can afford a robot's initial costs though.

The need to cut costs and the lack of skilled workers has driven many companies to out-source, causing countries in East Asia such as China and India to become the biggest threat to American manufacturing. The workers are not any more skilled, but they work longer hours for very cheap prices. Alan Tonelson, a writer for *The Wall Street Journal* explains in "Reviving Manufacturing" how, "It just makes good business sense. When you're talking about very labor-intensive industries like garment making, there's no shortage of even worse-paid workers" (Katel 606). Outsourcing jobs sounds good for business, but wreaks havoc on the already unemployed Americans and forces others into unemployment. According to the United States President's Council of Advisors on Science and Technology, some examples of products that were invented in the United States, but are now produced primarily abroad include laptop computers, solar cells, robotics, interactive electronic games and lithium-ion batteries ("Report" 5).

In the last few years however, good business sense is starting to favor American loca-tions. Senior Vice President Harold Sirkin of the Boston Consulting Group reported that wages in China are rising (Katel 605). The demand for a raise in payment shrinks the extra profit a company can earn by using cheap labor, driving them to stay or even return to the United States. But balancing costs aren't the only thing keeping companies in the United States, high quality products are also a factor. Raye explains that many products are created using a dye. An American dye will be more expensive initially, but will create more products than a cheaper dye made somewhere else before needing to be replaced. "China's method of mass producing doesn't ensure quality. It's a shotgun process. That's why you don't see the

Chinese making airplanes," he tells me over the phone. To ensure quality, many companies are focusing on Six Sigma; a method using math to prove only one in a million parts created with your process will be bad. One in a million is the current acceptable standard for quality, where it previously may have been one part in a hundred. Companies must decide individually how to balance the tradeoff of quality versus quantity. Raye elaborates by saying "A manufacturing engineer's job is to give them the best of both, high quality at high rates of production." Developing new systems for increased product production doesn't happen overnight and can be extremely complicated.

Educating more engineers seems like a simple solution to an overwhelming problem, but sometimes the easiest things are the hardest to do. Government data shows that in the United States, "math, engineering, technology and computer science students accounted for about 11.1 percent of college graduates in 1980 . . . [dropping] to about 8.9 percent in 2009" (Mutikani). The change can be credited to a poor economy making it difficult to afford college, a lack of interest in pursuing a scientific degree and a lack of commitment for finishing. But promoting science in primary schools would reap benefits later on.

The strongest areas of industry growth are occurring in "healthcare and the scientific, technical and computer fields," and in the "development of environmentally friendly—'green'—energy industries" such as wind and solar (Mutikani; Katel 243). With the most openings occurring in fields of scientific concentration and development, the most basic solution requires our schools to not only focus in on science but to think creatively.

Across the United States, schools such as Cal Poly, with a "Learn by Doing" motto, are already leading the way. Former Lockheed Martin Chairman Norman Augustine explains how the American culture fosters innovation by placing an emphasis on "challenging the norm, creating new ideas, not accepting everything as given, [and] not being interested in learning by rote"(Price 28–9). Even President Obama spoke with workers at the Allison Transmission Corporation factory in Indianapolis about development:

> I don't want the new breakthrough technologies and the new manufacturing taking place
> in China and India. I want all those new jobs right here in Indiana, right here in the United
> States of America, with American workers, American know-how, American ingenuity.
> (Katel 605)

The United States contains the ability to not only sustain its place at the top, but to thrive. All that remains is for the American people to step up and accept the challenge. I truly believe we can succeed.

You shouldn't be forced into choosing a manufacturing related career if your interests lie elsewhere (and know that as a daughter to a manufacturing engineer and as a student pursuing a manufacturing engineering major I seem biased), but exposing children to it and putting a larger emphasis on science would help close the growing gap created as skilled workers retire with no one to take their place. In the current trend, those with education in manufacturing and industrial fields will never be without work. If that isn't incentive enough in an ever fluctuating economy, I don't know what is.

Roxanne Raye is a manufacturing engineering major.

Works Cited

Katel, Peter. "Reviving Manufacturing." *CQ Researcher*. 22 July 2011: 601–6. Web. 2 Nov. 2011.

———. "Vanishing Jobs." *CQ Researcher*. 13 Mar. 2009: 225–48. Web. 2 Nov. 2011.

Mutikani, Lucia. "So Many U.S. Manufacturing Jobs, So Few Skilled Workers." *Reuters*. Thomson Reuters, 12 Oct. 2011. Web. 2 Nov. 2011. <http://in.reuters.com/>

Price, Tom. "Science in America." *CQ Researcher*. 11 Jan. 2008: 25–48. Web. 2 Nov. 2011.

Raye, Steve. Phone Interview. 1 Nov. 2011.

"Report to the President on Ensuring American Leadership in Advanced Manufacturing." President's Council of Advisors on Science and Technology. *The White House*. June 2011. Web. <http://www.whitehouse.gov/>

CONSIDER THIS

- *Raye uses questions in her introduction to establish the essay's focus. Does this rhetorical strategy work? How do the questions bring the reader into the essay?*
- *How does the writer's use of sources throughout the essay affect her voice? How do these particular quotations build the writer's* ethos, *as well as the essay's* logos *and* pathos? *Does the writer strike an effective balance with all three appeals?*

Graffiti as Rhetoric

The British graffiti artist simply known as Banksy is known for reappropriating public spaces and turning them into temporary canvasses—a uniquely public rhetorical act. Sometimes the argument is explicit, sometimes implicit, but it's almost always satirical. Graffiti, by nature, is an act of protest against "the establishment." Some people regard it as simple vandalism, while others see it as art.

Which aspects of the following images most immediately capture your eye? While one image uses a visual and text and the other relies only on visuals, both make arguments about our sociopolitical atmosphere. How are Banksy's arguments bolstered by the use of visuals and text in conjunction with each other? Why do they draw your attention? And perhaps most importantly, what arguments are these images making?

My First Banksy
Photograph by Marya Figueroa

In the image above Banksy uses familiar icons—the peace sign and heart—but then revises them to suggest different meanings. Are the figures, a boy and a doctor, iconic themselves? How do the figures create an emotional connection with political messages? What would be lost if the figures were omitted? What other elements of protest do you see in these images?

What statement is Banksy making here about warfare, children, and the current world political climate?

The Banksy in North Beach
Photograph by Marya Figueroa

LOOK HERE

To learn more about Banksy, watch the 2010 documentary, Exit Through the Gift Shop. *Watch a trailer here: http://www.banksyfilm.com/index.html*

Appendices

Posts
Photograph by Marya Figueroa

Where to Get Help with Your Writing

Your Instructor's Office Hours

If you are struggling to understand a concept studied in class or are simply having a hard time choosing a topic for an essay, do not hesitate to meet with your instructor during his/her designated office hours (or make an appointment if those hours don't work with your schedule). Your instructor's office hours will be posted in the course syllabus.

First-year students are often too intimidated or anxious to meet one-on-one with their instructors, yet a short meeting with your instructor can make a major difference when it comes to being successful in a course. Do not wait until you receive low grades on an essay or feel overwhelmed in the course before asking for help. Your instructor will appreciate you taking a pro-active stance toward your progress in the course. Make it a point to ask for assistance when you need it.

The University Writing and Rhetoric Center

The University Writing and Rhetoric Center (UWRC) offers *free,* one-to-one consultations for *any class project* that requires an element of writing and rhetoric: reading, writing, speaking, and developing visual texts. Tutors are undergraduate and graduate students professionally trained both in a 300-level course on one-to-one conferencing and in subsequent workshops on writing and rhetoric in the disciplines. Tutors are available to help all Cal Poly students improve their writing skills.

Students may use the UWRC's services at any stage of the writing process, whether they are getting started on a project or editing at the final stages. Thirty-minute and sixty-minute tutoring sessions are available by appointment or on a first-come, first-served basis.

The Center serves students at two locations on campus: **Building 10, Room 138; and Room 202B of the Kennedy Library.**

Writing center tutors are prepared to assist you with the following:

- Understanding the expectations of an assignment
- Brainstorming and generating ideas
- Crafting a thesis
- Developing an argument
- Organizing points
- Researching and documenting sources
- Adhering to a required format
- Editing a final draft
- Reviewing grammar and punctuation
- Writing in all disciplines (e.g. lab reports, research papers, literary analyses, senior projects)

Keep in mind that writing center tutors do not simply proofread papers or provide students with a stamp of approval on an assignment. Instead, the goal of a tutoring session is to help students to gain new writing strategies and improve their writing skills so that they more successfully may complete writing tasks at Cal Poly and beyond.

The University Writing & Rhetoric Center
Right here. Write now!

Scheduling an appointment is easy. Simply visit http://www.calpoly.mywconline.com. Drop-in tutoring is also available.

Kennedy Library: Resources for English 133/134

Personal Help in Kennedy Library

Research Help Desk—room 111: Get in-person help from a LibRAT, specially-trained Cal Poly students who know how to help you find what you are looking for. LibRATs are very friendly and don't bite!

Phone Support: If you prefer to speak to someone, call 756-2649.

Chat Help: offered by LibRATs, librarians and Kennedy Library staff.

For help hours, information about the chat box, go to: http://lib.calpoly.edu/ask/

Research Resources

As a Cal Poly student, you have access to some very extensive resources and you should take advantage of them while you can. Now is your chance to move beyond Wikipedia.

Books

PolyCAT helps you locate books, journals, DVDs and more in Kennedy Library, available immediately.

Link+ helps you locate books and other materials in Kennedy and 50 other Libraries. They will arrive at the library for pick-up in 3–5 days

Articles

For the list of Most Useful Databases, go to: Kennedy Home Page > Articles > Most Useful Databases.

This list includes several databases useful for English 133/134 under headings that suggest their particular usefulness. These databases often include full-text. If you don't see PDF or HTML when you see a good article, click the **Find It** button, as this may lead you to the full text in another database. Most databases allow you to email yourself articles and citations. Some let you select for peer-reviewed results.

Research Guides

English 134: links to catalogs, databases and resources relevant to this course.
Freshmen 101: general introduction to the library, designed in part for English 133/134. It also includes a tutorial on the research process.

Online Citation Help

Citation examples based on MLA 7th edition are available online at: http://lib.calpoly.edu/research/citations/mla.html

The MLA 7th edition is available at the Research Help Desk and at the Circulation (front) desk, call # LB2369 .G53 2009.

The OWL at Purdue provides excellent MLA examples and aid: http://owl.english.purdue.edu/owl/resource/747/01/

You can also seek individual help with citation at the **Research Help Desk, room 111.**

Key Research Vocabulary for English 133/134

Abstract: a brief description of the contents of an article.

Citation: information about a book or article that minimally includes author, title, date, and publisher.

Citation style: there are many formats for citation, such as MLA, Chicago, APA, etc. English 134 uses MLA.

Call Number: Library of Congress classification codes. The unique combination of letters and numbers tells you where a book is found among similar items. To find which floor your book is on, look at a library map.

Peer-Reviewed Journal: a journal that publishes articles only after they have been subjected to critique by multiple scholars in that field. Signs that an article is peer-reviewed are the presence of many citations, a text-heavy appearance, and academic affiliations of the editors and authors. If you are uncertain, one way to be sure is to visit the home page of the journal. Peer-reviewed journals are usually proud of the fact and announce it there.

Plagiarism: not giving proper credit for information to its source; copying someone else's ideas and passing them off as your own. In other words, don't cut and paste, or paraphrase, without giving credit.

For other information about the Library, use the Kennedy Home Page quick search box, and select for Website Content. http://lib.calpoly.edu/

This section was contributed by Brett Bodemer, Humanities and Social Sciences Librarian at Robert E. Kennedy Library.

Disability Resource Center

If you have been diagnosed with a learning disability, or are concerned that you may have an undiagnosed disability that is affecting your academic performance, contact Cal Poly's Disability Resource Center for further assistance (http://drc.calpoly.edu/).

English as a Second Language Students

The Cal Poly Composition Program is committed to placing students into writing courses that will best support them. Students for whom English is a second (or even third) language may want to consider taking writing classes that are intended to address their needs and talents.

To decide if such a writing course will benefit you, please consider the following:

- Do you speak a language other than English at home?
- Do your parents speak a language other than English at home?
- Did your previous instructors suggest that you might benefit from second-language support?
- Do you struggle when reading long, complex texts that are written in English?

If you are interested in taking a course that supports second-language students, please see the description of ENGL 133 below. Or, if you would like to work with a tutor who has training in working with students for whom English is not their first language, please contact the University Writing and Rhetoric Center (see above).

Defining and Avoiding Plagiarism

Cal Poly and the English Department prohibits cheating or academic dishonesty in any form.

Defining Plagiarism

Cal Poly's Campus Administrative Manual 684.3 states: "Plagiarism is defined as the act of using the ideas or work of another person or persons as if they were one's own without giving proper credit to the source. Such an act is not plagiarism if it is ascertained that the ideas were arrived through independent reasoning or logic or where the thought or idea is common knowledge. Acknowledgement of an original author or source must be made through appropriate references; i.e., quotation marks, footnotes, or commentary. Examples of plagiarism include, but are not limited to the following: the submission of a work, either in part or in whole completed by another; failure to give credit for ideas, statements, facts or conclusions which rightfully belong to another; failure to use quotation marks when quoting directly from another, whether it be a paragraph, a sentence, or even a part thereof; close and lengthy paraphrasing of another's writing without credit or originality; use of another's project or programs or part thereof without giving credit."

In other words, plagiarism occurs when, without proper citation, you quote the source's words exactly, use his or her images or audio files, or restate the source's ideas in your own words. Submitting without the knowledge or permission of your instructor a paper for one class that you have written for another class (including work written for your high school classes) is considered "self-plagiarism" and could result in penalty. Purchasing or downloading essays is also a form of plagiarism since the work you hand in is not your own.

You may have previously learned "rules" which tell you that you don't need to use quotation marks or to cite your source unless you "borrow" at least four consecutive words—but anytime you use words and ideas that are not your own, you will be expected to cite the source.

Examples of Plagiarism

- The submission of another person's work in any medium, either in part or as a whole, without acknowledgement
- Failure to give credit for ideas, statements, facts, or conclusions that rightfully belong to another person
- Failure to use quotation marks when quoting directly from another source whether the quotation is a paragraph, a sentence, or a phrase
- Paraphrasing (putting in your own words) another person's work without acknowledging that person as the author
- Including images, chart, graphs, etc. in your essay without properly citing the original source material (i.e. Google images)
- Submitting your written work for another class unless you have the express permission of both instructors

Note that quotation marks, signal phrases, and parenthetical citations generally address these problems.

Reading *Fresh Voices* Essays that Cite Sources

As you read the essays in this collection, focus on how students use sources to support their own ideas. In particular, note how they introduce and quote sources, how they paraphrase, summarize, and integrate quotations with signal phrases. In addition, don't skip over the works cited page at the end of essays. Rather, focus on how this page supplements the essay: every source cited in the essay (including images) needs to appear here. Learning how to incorporate and cite sources properly helps to build your credibility with your readers. While you may learn a different citation style in your major, the key is to know how to work with outside sources. Once you understand the basic principles for incorporating research sources, you will be able to adapt to any citation style.

The Consequences

According to university policy, as a student at Cal Poly, you are responsible for your actions. English 134 instructors have clearly stated plagiarism policies on their syllabi. **It is your responsibility to become familiar with these policies on plagiarism.**

Upon discovery of any form of academic dishonesty, you will be subject to a penalty as determined by the instructor (you may fail the assignment; you may fail the course). In addition, a report detailing the incident of academic dishonesty as well as the penalty determined by the instructor will be filed with the Office of Student Rights and Responsibilities.

According to the Office of Student Rights and Responsibilities, "Cheating requires, at a minimum, an 'F' assigned to the assignment, exam, or task, and this 'F' must be reflected in the course grade. The instructor may assign an 'F' course grade for an incidence of cheating."

WORK CITED

"Plagiarism." Office of Student Rights and Responsibilities. Consulted 17 June 2012. < http://www.osrr.calpoly.edu/plagiarism/>.

General Education Course Objectives

The General Education Course Objectives for English 133 and 134 state that as a student enrolled in the course, you will learn to:

1. Understand the writing act as a means of exploring and expressing your ideas.

2. Approach the act of writing as a recursive process that includes drafting, revising, editing and proofreading.

3. Develop and apply a rhetorical awareness of your audience and use that awareness to assess your audiences and adjust your utterances to that audience.

4. Understand major organizational strategies and apply those strategies effectively with reference to your audiences.

5. Become aware of the major stylistic options such as voice, tone, figurative language and point of view and apply these options with rhetorical appropriateness.

6. Apply the above objectives so as to write essays that are unified, coherent, and free of significant grammar, usage, punctuation, mechanics and spelling errors.

7. Read critically in such a way as to understand and to derive rhetorical principles and tactics that you can apply in writing and in critical reading of other students' papers.

8. Apply all of the above principles to in- and out-of-class original writing of not fewer than **4,000 words.**

English 133 and 134 emphasize a process approach to composition: instructors will engage in a dialogue with you about your writing and will provide feedback designed to prompt you to rethink your work. You will gain competence as a writer by learning how to assess your own work. In addition, English 134 is rhetorically oriented, which means you will learn to account for the relationship between writers, readers, and texts when you write.

Composition at Cal Poly:
Catalog Course Descriptions

The following courses constitute the composition curriculum at Cal Poly.

ENGL 102 Basic Writing II (4) (CR/NC)

Instruction in the writing process. Practice in the strategies of writing, revising, and editing paragraphs and essays with attention paid to focus, support, and organization. Directed readings of exemplary prose. Not for baccalaureate credit. Credit/No Credit grading only. Repeatable. 4 lectures.

Next Course in Sequence: ENGL 134

ENGL 113 Essay Writing/ESL (4) (CR/NC)

Practice in essay writing with special attention paid to the writing process. Focus on using details and examples for effective development. Review of grammar problems specific to ESL students. Journal writing to enhance fluency. Directed readings of essays and fiction. Not for baccalaureate credit. Credit/No Credit grading only. 4 lectures. Prerequisite: ENGL 111 or ENGL 112, or consent of instructor.

Next Course in Sequence: ENGL 133

Note: All ENGL 102 and 113 courses have been "stretched," which means that students in these courses continue to work with the same group of students and the same instructor in ENGL 133/134.

ENGL 103 Writing Laboratory (1) (CR/NC)

Directed practice in writing in a laboratory environment. Required of all students scoring below 147 on the English Placement Test (EPT). Not for baccalaureate credit. Credit/No Credit grading only. To be taken concurrently with the ENGL 133 and 134 parts of the stretch sequences.

ENGL 133 Writing and Rhetoric for English as a Second Language Students (4) GE A1

Writing and stylistic analysis of expository papers. Study and application of techniques of exposition. Critical reading of model essays. Special emphasis on grammar and writing issues appropriate for English as a Second Language students. 4 lectures. Prerequisite: ENGL 111, 112, or 113 or consent of instructor.

Next Course in Sequence: ENGL 145, 148, or 149

ENGL 134 Writing and Rhetoric (4) GE A1

Writing and stylistic analysis of expository papers. Study and application of techniques of exposition. Critical reading of models of effective writing. 4 lectures. Prerequisite: Satisfactory score on the English Placement Test.

Next Course in Sequence: ENGL 145, 148, or 149

ENGL 145 Reasoning, Argumentation, and Writing (4) GE A3

(Also listed as HNRS/SCOM 145) (formerly ENGL 215)
The principles of reasoning in argumentation. Examination of rhetorical principles and responsible rhetorical behavior. Application of these principles to written and oral communications. Effective use of research methods and sources. 4 lectures. Prerequisite: Completion of GE Area A1 with a C- or better, or consent of instructor. Recommended: Completion of GE Area A2.

ENGL 148 Reasoning, Argumentation and Technical Writing (4) GE A3

(Also listed as HNRS 148) (Replacement for ENGL 218)
The principles of reasoning in technical writing. Discussion and application of rhetorical principles, both oral and written, in technical environments. Study of methods, resources and common formats used in corporate or research writing. 4 lectures. Prerequisite: Completion of GE Area A1 with a C- or better, or consent of instructor. Recommended: Completion of GE Area A2.

ENGL 149 Technical Writing for Engineers (4) GE A3

(Also listed as HNRS 149) (Engineering replacement for ENGL 218)
The principles of technical writing. Discussion and application of rhetorical principles in technical environments. Study of methods, resources and common formats used in corporate or research writing. 4 lectures. Prerequisite: Completion of GE Area A1 with a C- or better, or consent of instructor. Recommended: Completion of GE Area A2. For Engineering students only. Cross listed as ENGL/HNRS 149. Fulfills GE A3.

The Graduation Writing Requirement

In 1976, the Trustees of the California State University System responded to both business community and university demands to reverse the decline in graduating students' writing skills. They stated that all students seeking a Bachelor's or Master's degree must "be required to demonstrate their proficiency with regard to writing skills as a requirement for graduation." The Trustees also decreed that students' writing skills be tested after completing ninety-quarter units.

Thus, the California State University System established the Graduation Writing Requirement to assure that students have maintained the ability to write proficiently at the time of graduation and before they enter the professional workforce.

Cal Poly responded positively to the Trustees' mandate and created two options for fulfilling the Graduation Writing Requirement (GWR):

1. Pass the Writing Proficiency Exam (WPE), which costs $35 and is given at 9 a.m. on a Saturday early in the fall, winter, and spring quarters. You must earn a score of 8 out of 12-points in order to complete your GWR milestone.

2. Pass a GWR-approved upper-division course with a grade of C or better AND receive certification of proficiency in writing based on a 500-word in-class essay. Students can enroll in one of the following NON-GE WRITING courses: English 301, 302, 310, 317, 318, 326; or from these GE C4 LITERATURE courses: 330, 331, 332, 333, 334, 335, 339, 340, 341, 342, 343, 345, 346, 347, 349, 350, 351, 352, 354, 370, 371, 372, 380, or 381.

The University has established GWR certification standards and specification guidelines, which must be met within the English courses in Option 2. If a student chooses Option 2 to meet the GWR, he or she must inform the instructor teaching that course and students may attempt to write a proficient in-class essay more than once.

When you reach ninety-quarter units, you can either take a GWR-approved upper-division course or you can take the WPE. During the summer quarter, course work is the only option available. Test dates and sign-up deadlines are published in the test section of the Student Planning Calendar in the Class Schedule.

Submitting Your Work to *Fresh Voices*

Fresh Voices 2013-2014 needs your essays and images!

- Are proud of essays you wrote in ENGL 134?
- Are you interested in photography, painting, or drawing?
- Do you want hundreds and hundreds of next year's freshmen to see your work?
- Do you want to tell future employers that you are PUBLISHED?

If so, submit your work to *Fresh Voices!*

We will accept ANY essays you completed for your ENGL 133, 134, 102, or 113 class. We will also accept any original artwork that could be appropriate for the collection.

If your essay is selected **you will receive a free copy of the collection, a certificate of achievement, and a gift certificate to a local business.**

What if Sesame Street had mailboxes?
Photograph by Marya Figueroa

What to submit

- Any work you completed in ENGL 134 or 102. You may submit as many pieces as you like.
- Essays ranging from 2-7 pages in length.
- All citations. We will not consider work that that does not properly cite sources
- Your draft material (optional). (Consider submitting your drafts—complete with instructor and/or peer comments—along with your final hard copy. We are unconcerned with grades and will not include them in the collection.)

How to Submit

1) Fill out a release form (posted here: http://cla.calpoly.edu/engl_freshvoices.html).
2) Email a copy of the essay to engl-freshvoices@calpoly.edu. (Please write **"FV"** in the subject line.)
3) Turn in hard copies of your work and the permission form to **47–35F.**

Essays must be received by the last day of finals week in spring quarter to be considered for publication. Please contact me if you have questions. The *Fresh Voices* select committee looks forward to reading your work!

> Dr. Brenda Helmbrecht
> Department of English
> Director of Writing